Ending Poverty: A 20/20 Vision

See www.lutheranvoices.com

LUTHERAN

VOICES

Ending Poverty: A 20/20 Vision
A Guide for Individuals and Congregations

Nancy Maeker
Peter Rogness

Augsburg Fortress

Minneapolis

ENDING POVERTY: A 20/20 VISION
A Guide for Individuals and Congregations

Large-quantity purchases or custom editions of these books are available at a discount from the publisher. For more information, contact the sales department at Augsburg Fortress, Publishers, 1-800-328-4648, or write to: Sales Director, Augsburg Fortress, Publishers, Box 1209, Minneapolis, MN 55440-1209.

Editor: Andrea Lee

Cover Design: © Koechel Peterson and Associates, Inc., Minneapolis, MN
www.koechelpeterson.com

Cover photo: © C. Sherburne/PhotoLink/PhotoDisc. Used by permission.

Library of Congress Cataloging-in-Publication Data
Maeker, Nancy, 1944-
  Ending poverty : a 20/20 vision : a guide for individuals and congregations / Nancy Maeker, Peter Rogness.
      p. cm.
ISBN-13: 978-0-8066-8003-3
ISBN-10: 0-8066-8003-2 (pbk. : alk. paper)
  1. Church work with the poor—Evangelical Lutheran Church in America. 2. Christian sociology—Evangelical Lutheran Church in America. I. Rogness, Peter. II. Title.
BX8074.B4M34 2006
261.8'325—dc22   2006007492

The paper used in this publication meets the minimum requirements of American National Standard for Information Sciences—Permanence of Paper for Printed Library Materials, ANSI Z329.48-1984.

Manufactured in the U.S.A.

10   09   08   3   4   5   6   7   8   9   10

Dedicated to the congregations

of the Saint Paul Area Synod—ELCA,

those committed to "A Minnesota Without Poverty,"

and all who are committed to ending poverty

Contents

Preface

Because . . .
God created humankind in the image of God. (Genesis 1:27)

Hebrew Scripture states that "if there is among you anyone in need, a member of your community, . . . do not be hard-hearted or tight-fisted toward your needy neighbor. . . . Open your hand to the poor and needy neighbor in your land" (Deuteronomy 15:7, 11).

Jesus said that any action done to one of the least of these who are members of his family is also action done to him. (Matthew 25:40)

God loved us first, and the question is, "How does God's love abide in anyone who has the world's goods and sees a brother or sister in need and yet refuses help?" (1 John 3:17).

Therefore . . .
A moral society protects the human dignity of all people.
The measure of a people—and the measure of our faith—is how well we care for those living in poverty.

So . . .
The first question to be asked and answered before making any decision—either personal or public—is this:

How will the decision or action affect those living in poverty?

Poverty and people of faith

Standing against poverty is nothing new, especially for Lutherans. Over the years, we have launched social ministries that serve the poor. We have responded to disasters. We have established food pantries and agencies like Lutheran Social Service. We have condemned occasionally the comfort and complacency with which followers of Christ have made peace with the existence of the poor at their doorstep. We have felt some chagrin at other people's insensitivity to the homeless here and the famines abroad. However, we are not a church made up of many poor people. In this country, Lutherans have settled into the comfort of third and fourth generations of immigrants, most all of us comfortably middle class. We are largely distant from these issues. We may sympathize with those seeking to eliminate poverty through advocacy, but such sympathies do not consume much of our attention and energy.

For ten years as a parish pastor, I (Peter) served a wonderful, mostly African American congregation in Milwaukee that was no stranger to persons living in poverty. For this congregation, walking with the poor was less a burden than a gift. Ministry was a gift in setting before us the strength, generosity, and resilience of people living in the grips of poverty. At the same time, the cruelty we inflict on each other as a human family and the sinfulness of tolerating the existence of the conditions that leave people in poverty was laid bare. The existence of poverty is unmistakably a faith issue when seen that up-close.

The emergence of "A Common Foundation"

In April 2002, I was elected bishop of the Saint Paul Area Synod. Most bishop elections include the question to nominees that goes something like, "What's your vision for this synod?" Here it was different. In 2001, after a discernment/planning process of years, the synod had adopted as one facet of its "Three-fold Vision for Mission" the following:

ensure that no person in the St. Paul area is forced to live in poverty

So the question to nominees here was, "What would you bring to the synod's three-fold vision?" It was a vision widely known and affirmed by the clergy and lay leaders throughout the synod. I was pleased that there was in place such a clear vision for the church's role in the world. In the ELCA's third largest synod (157,000 baptized members, three of the six largest ELCA congregations [ELCA Office of Research and Evaluation]), this represents enormous potential for having significant impact.

Overseeing the work of the synod's efforts to end poverty resides in a leadership team made up of clergy and lay leaders. (Specific details about how the leadership team is organized and the strategies it has employed to carry out its efforts follow in the appendix.) Because of its charge to work as a "catalyst for mission," the Ending Poverty team recognized from its inception that its work on this issue placed it in a posture of collaboration with others who share this commitment.

There is nothing uniquely Lutheran about concern for the poor. An idea emerged for a brief statement of principles held in common by a wide array of faith groups. I offered to prepare a draft and run it by other faith leaders for their input and support. Archbishop Harry Flynn, Catholic Archdiocese of Saint Paul and Minneapolis, liked both the idea and the draft and took it to the other Catholic bishops in Minnesota. I worked through the Minnesota Council of Churches to bring in additional Protestant judicatory leaders, and I made other contacts, every time resulting in suggestions and support and broadening the group to include Jewish, Muslim, and Hindu leaders in the state.

What struck the responsive chord among everyone was this: In all these traditions, stated variously but unmistakably parallel, the measure of our faithfulness to God is the extent to which our lives are lives of compassion and service, especially to those most in need.

Or, to state it even more clearly: In all these traditions, the measure of faithfulness is our treatment of the poor, the stranger, the outcast, the marginalized, the widow, and the orphan. Such measure is articulated in the sacred writings of each of these faith traditions and others besides. Addressing the needs of those living in poverty is not a narrow interest of a few people in a congregation. Rather, it is inherent in the very living out of the faith; it is foundational to the faithful life.

So was born the document known as "A Common Foundation: Shared Principles for Work on Overcoming Poverty." On March 31, 2004, fourteen leaders of religious bodies in the state of Minnesota gathered in the chancery of the offices of Catholic Archdiocese just across the street from the Cathedral of Saint Paul and overlooking the State Capitol and the city of St. Paul to sign their name to these principles. An additional twenty who were unable to be present signed the document later. By signing our name, each of us indicated that these commitments lie at the center of our understanding of what it means to be people of faith

In the next few pages, we will examine these shared principles briefly. The rest of this book provides a guide for groups in congregations that choose to more intentionally live out this commitment to the holy work of overcoming poverty.

"A Common Foundation: Shared Principles for Work on Overcoming Poverty"

Peter Rogness

As a people of faith, with varying theologies and traditions, we are convinced of a remarkable convergence on fundamental principles that call us to common work in combating poverty and walking with people living in poverty.

We believe it is the Creator's intent that all people are provided those things that protect human dignity and make for healthy life: adequate food and shelter, meaningful work, safe communities, healthcare, and education.

We believe we are intended to live well together as a whole community, seeking the common good, avoiding wide disparities between those who have too little to live on and those who have a disproportionate share of the world's goods.

We believe we are all called to work to overcome poverty and that this work transcends both any particular political theory or party and any particular economic theory or structure. We believe that overcoming poverty requires the use of private and public resources.

We believe we are called to make alliances within the faith community and with others in society who share the commitment to overcome poverty.

We believe that overcoming poverty involves both acts of direct service to alleviate the outcomes of poverty and advocacy to change those structures that result in people living in poverty.

We believe government is neither solely responsible for alleviating poverty, nor removed from this responsibility. We believe government is the vehicle by which people order their lives based on their shared vision. We believe society is well served when people of faith bring their values into the public arena. It is this remarkable convergence around issues of poverty and the common good that leads people of varying faith traditions to unite in calling on government to make a critical commitment to overcoming poverty.

We believe the desire to overcome poverty is not simply a human idea, but is the desire of our Creator, and that the work to create a more just and whole society will be empowered by the Creator's presence.

We invite each faith tradition to make explicit their expression of faith and how it understands this common foundation. On these shared principles, we together commit ourselves to work to ensure that no person is forced to live in poverty. (Copyright © 2004, Saint Paul Area Synod, Evangelical Lutheran Church in America. All rights reserved. Permission to reproduce granted.)

Bishop Jon Anderson
Southwestern Minnesota Synod, ELCA

Bishop Victor H. Balke
Roman Catholic Diocese of Crookston

Rev. Ian D. Bethel Sr., President
Minnesota Baptist Conference,
National Baptist Conference, Inc.

Rev. Connie Burkholder,
District Executive
Northern Plains District,
Church of the Brethren

Auxiliary Bishop Frederick F. Campbell
Roman Catholic Archdiocese
of Saint Paul and Minneapolis

Rev. Peg Chemberlin,
Executive Director
Minnesota Council of Churches

Rev. Larry Christianson, President
Western District of the Moravian Church

Rev. Sally Dyck, Bishop
Minnesota Annual Conference,
United Methodist Church

Rev. Diane Ehr, Associate Regional
Minister, Mid-American Baptists

Dr. Hamdy El-Sawaf, Executive
Director, Islamic Center of Minnesota

Archbishop Harry J. Flynn
Roman Catholic Archdiocese
of Saint Paul and Minneapolis

Dr. Richard Guentert, Regional Minister
Christian Church (Disciples of Christ)
of the Upper Midwest

Bishop Bernard J. Harrington
Roman Catholic Diocese of Winona

Bishop John Hopkins
Minnesota Annual Conference,
United Methodist Church President,
Minnesota Council of Churches

Bishop James Jelinek
Episcopal Diocese of Minnesota,
Episcopal Church USA

Bishop Craig Johnson
Minneapolis Area Synod, ELCA

Rev. Sharon Johnson, Executive Presbyter
Presbytery of Northern Waters,
Presbyterian Church USA

Bishop John F. Kinney
Roman Catholic Diocese of St. Cloud

Rev. Judith Kolwicz, Executive Presbyter
Presbytery of the Twin Cities,
Presbyterian Church USA

Rev. David MacMahill,
Conference Minister, Minnesota
Conference, United Church of Christ

Bishop John C. Nienstedt
Roman Catholic Diocese of New Ulm

Auxiliary Bishop Richard E. Pates
Roman Catholic Archdiocese of Saint
Paul and Minneapolis

Rev. Mark Peters, Lutheran Coalition
for Public Policy in Minnesota

Rev. Wayne Purintun, Executive Presbyter
Presbytery of Minnesota Valleys,
Presbyterian Church USA

Bishop Peter Rogness
Saint Paul Area Synod, ELCA

Mr. Vic Rosenthal
Jewish Community Action

Dr. Shashikant M. Sane
Hindu Mandir

Bishop Dennis M. Schnurr
Roman Catholic Diocese of Duluth

Mr. Stephen Silberfarb, Executive Director
Jewish Community Relations Council
of Minnesota and the Dakotas

Rev. Grant Stevenson

ISAIAH
Bishop Peter Strommen
Northeastern Minnesota Synod, ELCA

Rev. Charles Traylor, Executive Presbyter
Presbytery of Northern Plains,
Presbyterian Church USA

Bishop Harold Usgaard
Southeastern Minnesota Synod, ELCA

Bishop Rolf Wangberg
Northwestern Minnesota Synod, ELCA

(As of May 25, 2005)

A Commentary on

"A Common Foundation: Shared Principles for Work on Overcoming Poverty"

Peter Rogness

As a people of faith, with varying theologies and traditions, we are convinced of a remarkable convergence on fundamental principles that call us to common work in combating poverty and walking with people living in poverty.

We American Christians are blessed to live in a time of both proximity and openness to faith traditions other than our own. The ecumenical movement of the past half-decade has brought Christians to a point of discovering far greater areas of agreement and commonality than differences. Increased interfaith dialogues and relationships have opened to us not only spiritual insights but also shared values. While not abandoning or compromising the truth claims of our own deeply held religious convictions, we have been led to be open to the possibility that the God we know in Jesus Christ may have revealed something of the divine nature in other religious traditions as well. We have discovered that our religious teachings have vast and profound commonalities in how we are to live.

The "remarkable convergence" our document speaks of is just that. The written witness of Scripture—the words of Jesus and the Old Testament prophets—makes clear that the truest measure of our devotion to God lies in the compassion we show to the poor, the outcast, and the stranger, the "least of these." Interfaith dialogue has shown us that same truth present in other traditions as well. Peace, justice, and compassion reside as universal values in the world's great religions. Islamic leaders were immediately insistent that the attacks of September 11 and the work of religious extremists were a corruption of the teachings of Islam.

In this country, we have inherited the great tradition of the First Amendment, prohibiting the state from interfering in the world of religion or establishing and enforcing any one religion. It has helped keep the world of religion away from the corruption of temporal power. But an unfortunate side effect—itself a corruption of our religion—is the strong pattern of keeping faith out of the public arena, of not mixing religion with politics. For our own religious tradition, Lutheran Christianity, that separation is itself a serious error. Our faith is deeply personal, but never intended to be private. We proclaim a public faith for the world, both in witnessing to our belief in God's presence in our lives and in seeking to be advocates and builders of a human community that lives out these central values of peace, justice, and compassion. Ours is not an imperative to love only the neighbor who lives next door, but to exude the will for justice for the poor and outcast in every arena of life, both personal and public.

It's a fundamental human value we share with others in this remarkable convergence. Here is a sampling of what our faiths say about the care of those living in poverty:

From Hebrew Scripture

"I hate, I despise your festivals, and I take no delight in your solemn assemblies. Even though you offer me your burnt-offerings and grain-offerings, I will not accept them. . . . But let justice roll down like waters, and righteousness like an ever-flowing stream" (Amos 5:21-22, 24).

"He has told you, O mortal, what is good; and what does the LORD require of you but to do justice, and to love kindness, and to walk humbly with your God?" (Micah 6:8).

From Christian Scripture

"I was hungry and you gave me food. . . . I was a stranger and you welcomed me. . . . I was naked . . . sick . . . in prison. . . . As you did it to one of the least of these who are members of my family, you did it to me. . . . As you did not do it to one of the least of these, you did not do it to me." (Matthew 25:34-35)

"How does God's love abide in anyone who has the world's goods and sees a brother or sister in need and yet refuses help?" (1 John 3:17).

From Muslim Scripture

"Whoever saved a life, it would be as if he saved the life of all mankind."

From Hindu proverb

"They who give have all things; they who withhold have nothing."

From the Sikh holy book

"Those who remember God generously help others." (Guru Granth Sahib)

From Buddhist writings

"An offering given from what little one has is worth a thousand times its value." (Buddha)

*   *   *   *   *

We believe it is the Creator's intent that all people are provided those things that protect human dignity and make for healthy life: adequate food and shelter, meaningful work, safe communities, healthcare, and education.

The last 250 years of human history have seen the emergence of democracy as a form of government. There have been dozens of revolutions in which people have thrown off the yoke of oppression by kings and dictators to govern themselves. The documents that have undergirded these movements have spoken of the inherent dignity and worth of every human being. Our own Declaration of Independence exemplifies this: "We hold these truths to be self-evident, that all men are created equal, that they are endowed by their Creator with certain unalienable Rights, that among these are Life, Liberty, and the pursuit of Happiness. . . ."

The noblest of leaders in history called their followers to recognize what we now call basic human rights and embraced the worth of each life. We live in a flourishing of those values, when equality is understood to be the birthright of every person regardless of race, gender, age, nationality, ethnicity, sexual orientation, family status, language, or educational background. We in our faith tradition can claim it to be a flowering of our belief that we are all created in the image of God.

So what does it mean to take that idea, that value, from an abstract idea and put it into practice? We ascribe each person dignity and value, and in that we assume they have an inherent right to share in those things that make for healthy life:

- adequate food and shelter that provide for the basic needs of physical well-being;
- meaningful work that enables all persons to support themselves and their families and to be productive members of human society;
- safe communities that order our life together in ways that protect all from the harm or domination by others;
- health care that says the care of our bodies is not something for only the privileged;
- education that ensures all children have the chance to learn to live well in the world and develop their potential.

All these things together allow for each person to live as a valued member of the human community. Any of these things denied results in people unable to live with dignity as productive partners in the human family God has created.

*   *   *   *   *

We believe we are intended to live well together as a whole community, seeking the common good, avoiding wide disparities between those who have too little to live on and those who have a disproportionate share of the world's goods.

Christians have in recent years rediscovered the richness of the Old Testament Hebrew word, "shalom." We translate it as "peace," but its meaning suggests much more than a simple absence of conflict or war. Shalom points to wholeness, a proper balance, and harmonious fitting together of people and creation, a reflection of God's intent. While many themes in Scripture point to the battle between good and evil and call the people of God to triumph over forces of evil, such triumph is never for the purpose of dominance of one over another, for the amassing of power for personal gain or influence. Self-indulgence that leads to massive personal wealth and power unfailingly leads to strong condemnation because it upsets the balance of all lives having worth, violates the dignity of persons, and tears at the rich interweaving of the fabric of human community.

Our society celebrates the freedom and worth of the individual. Such a value on individualism reminds us that no institution or individual should amass power to trample others. An economic system that gives free reign to the efforts of individuals can result in the uneven amassing of wealth in the hands of a few, leaving the many struggling for basic needs. Adam Smith, recognized as the founder of free market capitalism, was a moral philosopher, not an economist. At the center of his thinking was the existence of "the invisible hand," the moral force that would restrain the flow of capital into a concentration that would eat away at the fabric of the whole of society.

We flirt with that moral danger today. Creation of wealth lifts the standard of living for all people, and this country has demonstrated an economic vigor that is the envy of other countries throughout the world. But such economic vigor has not necessarily made us admired around the world. The rest of the world is not sharing in this accumulation of wealth. Several years ago the Global Policy Forum published some disturbing statistics about these disparities ("Statistics on Poverty and Inequality," Jeff Gates, *Shared Capitalism Institute*, May 1999, viewed at www.globalpolicy. org/socecon/inequal/gates99.htm):

- The wealth of the three most well-to-do individuals exceeds the combined GDP of the forty-eight least-developed countries.
- In 1968, the people in well-to-do countries were thirty times better off than those in countries where the poorest 20 percent of the world's people live. In 1996 the gap was sixty-one times better off. In 1998, eighty-two times better off.
- The United Nations Development Program (UNDP) calculates that an annual 4 percent levy on the worlds 225 most wealthiest people would suffice to provide the following essentials for *all* those in developing countries: adequate food, safe water and sanitation, basic education, basic health care, and reproductive health care.
- In the United States: the wealth of the nation's top 1 percent was greater than the bottom 90 percent.

God's vision for human community calls us to act more justly and distribute the world's wealth more equitably, recognizing that the goal of all these efforts is not simply maximizing individual wealth and power, but maximizing the dignity and potential of every member of the human community God has created.

*   *   *   *   *

We believe we are all called to work to overcome poverty, and that this work transcends both any particular political theory or party and any particular economic theory or structure. We believe that overcoming poverty requires the use of private and public resources.

Zeal and energy over issues related to poverty have been wasted in false arguments. Slogans such as "bleeding-heart liberal" or "compassionate conservative" do not further the discussion. The flip assumption that "anyone concerned about the poor must be a liberal" both insults conservatives and fails to hold liberals and conservatives alike accountable for their decisions.

As people of faith, we are called to fight against poverty. Period. Whether one is a Democrat or Republican, capitalist or socialist is not the point. The challenge for people of all political persuasions is to demonstrate how their theories and their policies advance the fight against poverty.

It is a false argument to fight over whether the poor are to be the concern of the private or public sector. People of faith must move in both arenas. If the living out of our life values puts us in a position of action on behalf of the poor, as it should, then such work will be expressed in both the public and private arenas.

For people of faith, any political party, any economic theory, and any sector of society must be judged on its effectiveness in contributing to a whole and healthy human community, especially as that community finds within it a place for the dignity and health of the poor. No sector, no party, no economic theory stands isolated from the person of faith seeking those ends.

*   *   *   *   *

We believe we are called to make alliances within the faith community and with others in society who share the commitment to overcome poverty.

Our own distinctive faith commitment is not diminished when we find convergence with others around any particular point. To find ourselves serving in a soup kitchen with Muslims leads us to discover the breadth of our concern for the hungry. To advocate for better social services with a group of disabled veterans or for special education funding with groups of immigrants reminds us of how fundamental these concerns are. In each case, we catch a glimpse of the vast presence and activity of the God who has awakened such commitments in us, also finding ways to awaken these commitments in others as well.

I remember years ago going to work on a Habitat house during Jimmy Carter Work Week. Cars parked for blocks meant I had to walk a distance, and I started noticing bumper stickers. I could not remember being anywhere that had seen such rich evidence of the full spectrum: politically conservative and liberal; pro- and anti-war; pro-choice and pro-life; school stickers from inner city and far-flung suburbs. All these people drove to the work site because of a shared commitment that people living in poverty ought to live in decent homes. A remarkable convergence. I think God was smiling.

*　*　*　*　*

We believe that overcoming poverty involves both acts of direct service to alleviate the outcomes of poverty and advocacy to change those structures that result in people living in poverty.

A story that surfaces in the course of church-based community organizing goes something like this: Someone living in a village along a river noticed the body of a person floating down river past the village and swam out to bring the person in. He and others gave medical care and began the path to healing. The next day, two more persons were found floating down river and again were rescued. This repeated itself each day, with the numbers growing.

It finally dawned on the people of the village that there was need for them to do something more than simply rescue and care for these people; they needed to move upriver, find and stop whatever it was that was causing the steady stream of dying victims. Their level of activity in seeking to rescue the people in the river was necessary and commendable, but so was the need to correct the conditions that produced the victims.

The reemergence of people of faith into the public arena has come about because of the rediscovery of the need for both kinds of involvement. People of faith, acting on their values of compassion and service, have long given care to the suffering. Before the recent emergence of health care conglomerates, many if not most of the hospitals in this country traced their roots to people of faith. Lutheran Services in America is the largest network of social-service providers in the country. We Lutherans have a long and proud history of direct service. The recent strategic planning process of the Evangelical Lutheran Church in America called on us to "step forward as a public church that witnesses boldly to God's love for all that God has created."

Increased advocacy in the public arena ought not be undertaken with the arrogance of exclusive claims to knowing God's will for specific legislation, but should be undertaken with the boldness of knowing that the call for us to love our neighbor is a call that inexorably draws us into that public arena, especially on behalf of those who have little voice.

*   *   *   *   *

We believe government is neither solely responsible for alleviating poverty, nor removed from this responsibility. We believe government is the vehicle by which people order their lives based on their shared vision. We believe society is well served when people of faith bring their values into the public arena. It is this remarkable convergence around issues of poverty and the common good that leads people of varying faith traditions to unite in calling on government to make a critical commitment to overcoming poverty.

The political mood in recent years has swung toward a diminishing role for government and a desire to increase the responsibility of the private sector. Politicians have recited a mantra of tax freezes or cuts. Public confidence in government has declined. Many people in all sectors have heard the call for the government to get out of the social service business and leave it to churches and charities.

In a large and complex age, however, the problem of scale emerges. Several years ago, an analysis of the effect of the proposed tax cuts for that year alone showed that every church budget in the country would have to double, with every new dime going for social services, just to cover the cuts proposed that year alone. Only the government can fill some of our needs. We do not leave our country's military security to churches and volunteer groups because the need is too great. If it becomes a shared value that people ought not to live imprisoned by poverty, then it becomes a shared value to use all means at our disposal—including government, but not government alone—to live out that value.

Politics is nothing more or less than the process by which we shape our life together. We choose what kind of people we want to be. In a democracy, we elect people to help create that kind of community. Legislators give shape to the morality that we wish to express and the way we want to live together. If our morality says we value all persons equally, then we shape a public life that does not give favor or privilege to a few, but enhances the dignity of all. If our values lead us to believe that each is entitled to life's basic needs, that children should be valued highly, or that recent immigrants deserve dignity, then politics is the means by which we become that kind of people.

Taxes are not inherently good or evil; they are simply the means we use to pool our resources to be who we wish to be as a people. When lawmakers consider whether to raise or lower taxes, they ought to first consider what we want to do and become. We first make decisions about the kind of people we want to be, the kind of place we want to shape for our common life. Then we make decisions about how to use our financial resources to shape that common life. We seek to help people at critical times in their lives. We recognize the needs of people who find themselves in circumstances where they need the help of others—the very young, the elderly, the poor, the immigrant, those thrust into crisis. It is both compassionate and enlightened public policy and—for those of us in the faith community, a God-pleasing thing to do—to see that such assistance is in place.

We do it as a moral people, both through our government—of, by, and for the people, after all—and through all other sectors of society where we have a voice.

*   *   *   *   *

We believe the desire to overcome poverty is not simply a human idea, but is the desire of our Creator, and that the work to create a more just and whole society will be empowered by the Creator's presence.

God's presence and mission is not simply in religious rites carried on in religious buildings. It is in the world. Nehemiah heeded the call to return to Jerusalem to rebuild the wall. William Pitt took the battle against slavery into the British Parliament for decades. Martin Luther King Jr. answered the call to march for equality in the streets of Birmingham. Dietrich Bonhoeffer was martyred for seeking to end Hitler's evil acts. Holy work is work in the world.

But because it is in the world does not make it any less holy, nor any less connected to the God who is, after all, creator and Lord of both heaven and earth, not just heaven and church. And in searching for God's intent for the shape of human community, nothing comes clearer than God's desire that humanity reaches out to its poorest members to end the withering grip of poverty. This is holy work.

We live in an age of shrill "wedge issues" that tear at the fabric of church and society alike. Abortion, sexuality, war—the pressures that divide are powerful, and the challenge to rise above the divisions is great.

Poverty presents another possibility. Working to end poverty has powerful potential to be a convergence issue. In the summer of 2005, just prior to the G-8 Conference on global poverty in Gleneagles, Scotland, I was part of a group of religious leaders who met in London. British Chancellor of the Exchequer Gordon Brown met with a group of two dozen religious leaders from the United States and the United Kingdom—Archbishop of

Canterbury Rowan Williams; American evangelicals Jim Wallis, Geoff Tunnicliffe, Richard Cizek, and Ron Sider; Catholics and mainline Protestants; and the presidents of Bread for the World and World Vision.

Chancellor Brown spoke of the Millennium Development Goals and suggested that the rich nations of the world now have the means to end hunger around the globe. "We have the means," he said. "What we lack is the moral will." Looking straight at us, he said, "That's your job."

Of course it is! Isn't it crystal clear that it is, as Micah said, "what God requires of us?" Unlike wedge issues, there is no argument here. This is not just our idea. It is God's idea. Crystal clear. And it is God's work, God's mission. So we ought not to be surprised as we set about this holy work to find the power of God sustaining us at every turn.

Introduction

Myrna Nelson, Saint Paul Area Synod council representative on the Ending Poverty Leadership Team, and I (Nancy) sat at the beachfront café having lunch with Ruby Payne. It was June 2003, and Myrna and I were attending the Training the Trainers week-long workshop in Galveston, Texas. Payne was teaching educators, administrators, nonprofit executives, a few business people, and another few church people—a gathering of more than three hundred from many parts of the country—about the culture of generational poverty and how to communicate to others an understanding of the culture of class, as well as an effective approach to teaching students who come out of generational poverty.

I had become aware of Ruby's "Framework for Understanding Poverty" when Pastor Cheryl Indehar, another member of the Ending Poverty team, had introduced me to Jodi Pfarr, a local consultant and workshop leader for Ruby Payne's material. We had sponsored Jodi for a major presentation at our synod assembly that same year, and we knew we needed to know more and be equipped to teach some of the material ourselves. Thus we had registered to attend the workshop in Galveston and hoped to have a direct conversation with Payne about our synod's initiative to end poverty in the Saint Paul area by 2010.

As Myrna and I talked with Ruby Payne on that bright June day, we told her about the Saint Paul Area Synod's vision for ending poverty in our area. Without a smile or any note of doubt, she told us directly, "Well, you can't end poverty in ten years, but you can in twenty years." She went on to map out the process by which to measure what an end of poverty would look like and plan the steps to get there.

We listened, took notes, asked questions, and understood the significance of her counsel. When we later reported the content of that conversation to the Ending Poverty Leadership Team, the effect was the clarifying of the synod's vision. Now we began to speak and write about the goal of *Ending Poverty: A 20/20 Vision*—with the intentional double meaning of 20/20 clarity of sight as well as by the year 2020.

How to use this book

This book is adaptable for individual or group use within the congregation or among congregations. While much of the content can be completed independently, small group discussions using the material will strengthen understanding, build community, and assist in developing action plans for your own congregation.

God's mission is always contextual; it takes place at a particular time and in a particular place or context. Therefore, while the subject of this book is poverty, each of the four chapters presents a particular congregational context:

Emmaus Lutheran, a first-ring suburb congregation
Second Lutheran, a city-neighborhood congregation
Christ the King Lutheran, a third-ring suburb congregation
St. John's Lutheran, a rural-urban fringe congregation

Chapter 1 What Is Poverty?	Emmaus Lutheran
Chapter 2 Communities of Poverty	Second Lutheran
Chapter 3 The Hidden Culture of Class	Christ the King Lutheran
Chapter 4 We Are One Community	St. John's Lutheran

Individual study

This book uses scenarios, Bible study, journaling, and other tools as a way to enter into issues and experience new learning. Additional reference material and Web site links provide access to a wealth of information that can deepen understanding and provide potential connections with others.

Group study

The material and format can be used by a congregational task force or class to facilitate depth of understanding of their situation as well as options for moving into action. Bible study, questions, data, and other information are provided to stimulate discussion and interaction.

1

What Is Poverty?

Debra's story

Debra knew her life seemed chaotic. When one thing started going right, three other parts of her life fell apart. As she wearily drove home from her second job, she thought about her situation. She remembered how her first husband had left her for another woman and the terrible effect that had had on her. She remembered how she would sit for hours in her old car outside of the woman's apartment, knowing her husband was inside; how she even thought about doing something drastic to herself or her husband or the other woman.

But that time had passed, and she knew her marriage to him had not been a healthy relationship from the start. She had moved to Dallas because her brother had found work here and had encouraged her to come. That was now eight years ago, and she and her two sons—and new baby daughter—were still here and her brother had moved back home. Sometimes she wondered whether she also should have gone back, but she knew the jobs were even more scarce there. But she worried about her mother back home, who was still working her cleaning job even though her health was failing and she ought to be slowing down now.

After she had moved here, she had met Al, who coached her sons' community football team. She had known he had some previous scrapes with the law, but he had been such a good influence on her sons that she had ignored his past history. Besides, she didn't know much about his situation anyway. And his mother lived in town and adored him as well as her and her two sons. So, they had married, and for a while things were looking very hopeful. They were both working and had bought a small home where the schools seemed to be good. The boys had led them to a new congregation because they had gotten involved with some of the sports activities there. She and Al at first had attended to find out what the boys were getting involved in, then had become involved themselves. Al had even been a volunteer with the youth group. And she became active in Sunday morning worship and Bible study.

But now, after breaking his parole, Al was back in prison, and she had a baby daughter in addition to her two sons. Al's mother was helping to care for little Mary, but Debra was working two full-time jobs and sometimes a third on weekends. She was always tired and had so little time for parenting. Her two sons were now teenagers, and she worried about them.

Debra's journal

Monday

I'm so tired I can hardly lift this pen, but I know I feel better when I write down my thoughts and prayers. This journal has really become my devotion time. Tonight on my drive home I wondered again where my life is headed. I guess I've been through a lot, but, God, I do believe the gospel hymn says it well: "You didn't bring me this far just to leave me." I want you to lead me.

Tuesday

Tonight on my drive home I had this powerful sense that you are leading me somewhere, God. Even when I'm exhausted from working two full-time jobs and a weekend part-time job and from worrying about the kids, I still think about going back to school. I know that is crazy, but the thought keeps coming anyway. I have the kids to support and if I quit one of my jobs, I can't make the house payments and all of the other bills. Here I go in this cycle again. There doesn't seem to be any good answer. Help me, God.

Wednesday

I am so angry and upset I don't know what to do! I came home at the usual time (11:00 P.M.) after my late job, and James wasn't home. He had left Mike in charge of taking care of Mary (a two-year-old!) and had gone out with friends. He thought he would get home before I did and I would never find out. I can't believe he would do that. I count on him. James knows that he needs to take care of Mike and Mary while I'm at my evening job. I know it's hard on him (after all he's just a teenager), but I can't expect Al's mother to take care of Mary all of the time. And to think I was considering going back to school! What a laugh!

Thursday

Okay now, I don't feel as angry and down as I did last night. In fact, I feel a bit hopeful. I decided to call my boss to tell him I would be late for work this morning. Then James and I had a good talk after breakfast and before he went to school. For the first time he told me how he does resent having to care for Mary—and Mike, for that matter—so much. However, he did say he was sorry about last night. He even confessed that he had gone out one other time and had made it back before I came home. That started to get me upset again, but, instead, I kept my cool and stayed calm. He told me that he really likes the youth group at church and resents not being able to play basketball with the rest of the youth on Wednesday nights. Well, later, after I got to work and had a bit of a lull, I called Pastor Carol and talked to her about what goes on at church on Wednesday evenings. I told her a bit about my situation, and she said that they had child care available on Wednesday nights, in addition to the other programs. She even said that she or one of the other adult leaders would be glad to pick up the kids and bring them home on

Wednesday evenings. I hadn't even thought about that possibility. But when I was telling MeMe (Al's mother) about this arrangement for Wednesdays, she insisted that she would keep Mary overnight on Wednesdays so the boys could go to church activities without having to take Mary along. Wow! I'm really thankful, God.

Friday

I know this may be silly, but on my way to my second job today I stopped by the community college and picked up some brochures. I also found out that they offer some night and weekend courses. I wonder.

Saturday

I worked my part-time job this morning, then crashed for a few hours. Then the kids and I went to the picnic and sports event sponsored by our church. We all had a great time, and it was so good to do something positive as a family. When we first started going to Emmaus Lutheran, I didn't think I would fit in, but now I do feel supported and accepted there. I even discovered two other women in similar situations as mine—single parents working hard to raise kids—and keep them out of trouble. We promised that we would keep in touch by phone and at church. But the best part of the whole evening was meeting "Auntie Martha" (that's what we started calling her) who loves children and offered to take care of Mary if I wanted to take a course next semester. God, are you telling me something?

Going deeper

Understanding poverty

The story about Debra (not her real name) is based on a true story. Debra came out of generational poverty—in which her grandparents had been sharecroppers in the old South, and her mother and stepfather had both worked in manual labor all of their lives. While Debra's situation is a challenging and sometimes exhausting one, there is also much hope. Here is why:

Educator, author, and consultant on the culture of poverty Ruby Payne, in *A Framework for Understanding Poverty*, defines poverty as "the extent to which an individual does without resources" (Highlands, Texas: aha! Process, Inc., 2001, p. 16). She then goes on to describe eight resources needed in people's lives:

Financial: having the money to purchase goods and services

Emotional: being able to choose and control emotional responses, particularly to negative situations, without engaging in self-destructive behavior

Mental: having the mental abilities and acquired skills (reading, writing, computing) to deal with daily life

Spiritual: believing in divine purpose and guidance

Physical: having physical health and mobility

Support systems: having friends, family, and backup resources available to access in times of need

Relationships/role models: having frequent access to adults who are appropriate, who are nurturing, and who do not engage in self-destructive behavior

Knowledge of hidden rules: knowing the unspoken cues and habits of a group

While Debra's situation was indeed grave, she either had or was in the process of developing all eight resources. Her challenging financial situation was related to the fact that, with her high school diploma and several college courses, she could only find low-wage jobs. Thus she was working two full-time jobs to make ends meet. However, she had the mental, physical, and spiritual resources to support her. Her congregation and her network of family and friends provided support systems, relationships, and role models. Because of her own resiliency, she was able to intuit the hidden rules that she needed to understand in order to succeed in the job and academic world to which she aspired.

Payne's definition for poverty provides a helpful tool with which to understand the situation of an individual as well as to analyze a community or a congregation. In considering Debra's situation, some resources are available to her already and some are in process. In looking at a congregation or a community, an analysis of resource accessibility can be determined by looking at availability of living-wage jobs, affordable housing, healthcare, transportation, support systems, health of schools, and the commitment of congregations to invite in and reach out to people of a variety of cultural and economic backgrounds.

Discovering the availability—or lack thereof—of resources in a congregation and community can provide clear implications for the mission to which God is calling a congregation. This research will uncover needs and opportunities for a congregation and the community in which it is located.

A different but somewhat similar definition of poverty is based on "A Common Foundation: Shared Principles for Overcoming Poverty," which originated in the Saint Paul Area Synod of the ELCA (see page 13). The definition implied in this document is that poverty is the lack of access to "those things that protect human dignity and make for healthy life: adequate food and shelter, meaningful work, safe communities, healthcare, and education."

As with Ruby Payne's definition, this definition of poverty also implies (1) ways to assess poverty for an individual or a community and (2) possible solutions for overcoming poverty for an individual or a community.

Statistics about poverty

The following sources provide some current statistics about poverty in the United States.

- The official poverty rate in 2004 was 12.7 percent, up from 12.5 percent in 2003. In 2004, 37.0 million people were in poverty, up 1.1 million from 2003.

- Poverty rates remained unchanged for Blacks (24.7 percent) and Hispanics (21.9 percent), rose for non-Hispanic Whites (8.6 percent in 2004, up from 8.2 percent in 2003), and decreased for Asians (9.8 percent in 2004, down from 11.8 percent in 2003).

- The poverty rate in 2004 (12.7 percent) was 9.7 percentage points lower than in 1959, the first year for which poverty estimates are available (Figure 3). From the most recent low in 2000, both the number and rate have risen for four consecutive years, from 31.6 million and 11.3 percent in 2000 to 37.0 million and 12.7 percent in 2004, respectively.

- For children under 18 years old, both the 2004 poverty rate (17.8 percent) and the number in poverty (13.0 million) remained unchanged from 2003. The poverty rate for children under 18 remained higher than that of 18- to 64-year-olds (11.3 percent) and that of people aged sixty-five and over (9.8 percent).

- Both the poverty rate and number in poverty increased for people 18 to 64 years old (11.3 percent and 20.5 million in 2004, up from 10.8 percent and 19.4 million in 2003).

- The poverty rate decreased for seniors aged 65 and older, 9.8 percent in 2004, down from 10.2 percent in 2003, while the number in poverty in 2004 (3.5 million) was unchanged. (Source: DeNavas-Walt, Carmen, Bernadette D. Proctor, and Cheryl Hill Lee, U. S. Census Bureau, Current Population Reports, p. 60-229, *Income, Poverty, and Health Insurance Coverage in the United States: 2004*, U. S. Government Printing Office, Washington, D. C., 2005.)

- In 2004, 45.8 million people in the United States were without health insurance coverage, up from 45.0 million people in 2003. The percentage of people covered by employment-based health insurance decreased to 59.8 percent in 2004, from 60.4 percent in 2003. With a 2004 uninsured rate at 18.9 percent, children in poverty were more likely to be uninsured than all children (Legal Momentum [August 2005], *Reading between the lines: Women's poverty in the United States, 2004,* accessed March 13, 2006, www.legalmomentum.org/womeninpoverty2004.pdf).

Poverty USA

The following statistics are gleaned from the Web site of the Catholic Campaign for Human Development: www.usccb.org/cchd/povertyusa:

- Twenty-nine percent of working families in the United States with one to three children under age twelve do not earn enough income to afford basic necessities like food, housing, health care, and childcare (Economic Policy Institute, 2001).
- Nearly 40 percent of America's poor over the age of sixteen worked either part-time or full-time in 2001—yet could not earn enough to secure even the basic necessities of life.
- Three out of four children in poverty lived with a family member who worked at least part time. And one out of every three children in poverty lived with someone who worked full-time, year round (Current Population Survey, U.S. Census Bureau, September 2002).
- A single parent of two young children working full-time in a minimum wage job for a year would make $10,712 before taxes—more than $4,300 below the poverty line (Current Population Survey, U.S. Department of Labor; U.S. Census Bureau, March 2001).
- The number of Americans living in poverty grew significantly in 2001, swelling to 32.9 million people—nearly one out of every eight people in the United States. Poverty's rise to 11.7 percent of the total population represented an additional 1.3 million people falling into need—and the first year-to-year rise in a decade (Current Population Survey, U.S. Census Bureau, September 2002).
- The top ten cities (100,000 or more population) with highest rate of child poverty (Census 2000, U.S. Census Bureau):

1. Brownsville, TX	45.3%
2. Hartford, CT	41.3%
3. New Orleans, LA	40.5%
4. Providence, RI	40.5%
5. Atlanta, GA	39.3%
6. Buffalo, NY	38.7%
7. Miami, FL	38.5%
8. Gary, IN	38.2%
9. Cleveland, OH	38.0%
10. Laredo, TX	38.0%

- The top 10 states with highest poverty rate, 2000–2001 (Current Population Survey, U.S. Census Bureau, 2002):

1. New Mexico	17.7%
2. Mississippi	17.1%
3. Arkansas	17.1%
4. District of Columbia	16.7%
5. Louisiana	16.7%
6. West Virginia	15.6%
7. Texas	15.2%
8. Oklahoma	15.0%
9. Alabama	14.6%
10. New York	14.0%

Bible study
Read Genesis 1:26-27 and Psalm 8.
- What do these passages say about God's stance toward all people? Toward each individual?

Read John 4:1-42.
- Let your imagination play with the story of the woman at the well. Try to assess which of the eight resources were available to her, which ones were not, and which ones are not even implied.

Read Matthew 25:31-40.

- Whom do you think of when you hear the phrase, "the least of these"?
- What does Jesus say about making resources accessible?

Read Acts 2:43-47.

- Think about how resources were shared in this scenario.
- Does this passage depict an imaginary idealistic community, or can we learn real-life behaviors from this community?

Read Acts 6:1-6.

- How were needs dealt with in the early church?
- What can we learn and apply to our congregation and our church as a whole?

Resources

The Christian Century 120, no. 12 (June 14, 2003). The theme for this issue is "The Widening Gap." See especially the article "Insufficient Funds: When Hard Work Doesn't Pay" by Marcia Z. Nelson, page 20.

Ehrenreich, Barbara. *Nickel and Dimed: On (Not) Getting by in America.* New York: Metropolitan Books, 2001.

Evangelical Lutheran Church in America Advocacy Ministries Web site: www.elca.org/advocacy

Lutheran Office for Governmental Affairs Web site: www.loga.org

Payne, Ruby K. *A Framework for Understanding Poverty,* Highlands, TX: aha! Process, Inc., 2001.

Payne, Ruby K. and Bill Ehlig. *What Every Church Member Should Know about Poverty.* Highlands, Texas: aha! Process, Inc., 1999.

Saint Paul Area Synod Web site: www.spas-elca.org/aboutsynod/poverty/endingpoverty.htm

Shipler, David. *The Working Poor: Invisible in America.* New York; Alfred A. Knopf, 2004.

Perspectives

My Name Is Not "Those People"

My name is not "Those People."
I am a loving woman, a mother in pain, giving birth to the future,
where my babies have the same chance to thrive as anyone.

My name is not "Inadequate."
I did not make my husband leave—he chose to,
and chooses not to pay child support.
Truth is, though, there isn't a job base for all fathers to support their
families.
While society turns its head, my children pay the price.

My name is not "Problem and Case to Be Managed."
I am a capable human being and citizen, not a client.
The social service system can never replace the compassion and concern
of loving grandparents, aunts, uncles, fathers, cousins, community—all
the bonded people who need to be but are not present to bring children
forward to their potential.

My name is not "Lazy, Dependent Welfare Mother."
If the unwaged work of parenting, homemaking, and community
building was factored into the Gross National Product, my work
would have untold value. And I wonder why my middle-class sisters
whose husbands support them to raise their children are
glorified—and they don't get called lazy and dependent.

My name is not "Ignorant, Dumb, or Uneducated."
I live with an income of $621 with $169 in food stamps.
Rent is $585. That leaves $36 a month to live on.
I am such a genius at surviving that I could balance the state budget
in an hour.

Never mind that there is a lack of living-wage jobs.
Never mind that it is impossible to be the sole emotional,
social, and economic support to a family.
Never mind that parents are losing their children to the gangs, drugs,
stealing, prostitution, social workers, kidnapping, the streets, the predator.
Forget about putting money into schools—just build more prisons.

My name is not "Lay Down and Die Quietly."
My love is powerful and my urge to keep my children alive will
never stop. All children need homes and people who love them.
They need safety and the chance to be the people
they were born to be.

The wind will stop before I let my children become a statistic.
Before you give in to the urge to blame me,
the blame that lets us go blind and unknowing into
the isolation that disconnects us, take another look.
Don't go away.
For I am not the problem, but the solution.
And . . . My name is not "Those People."
—*Julia Dinsmore* (Used by permission of the author.)

Key points about poverty

From *What Every Church Member Should Know about Poverty* by Ruby Payne and Bill Ehlig, pp. 11-12:

1. Poverty and wealth are relative. We basically know only our own poverty or wealth in relationship to others. Poverty in the United States was defined in 1993 as $14,763 or less for a family of four (annual income). In 1996, one was considered to be "marginally rich" if the household income was $70,000 or more a year.
2. Poverty occurs in all races and countries. In America in 1996, the largest group of individuals in poverty were children under the age of eighteen. According to the Center for the Study of Poverty

at Columbia University, 25 percent of all the children in America live in poverty. And if one counts the number of children very close to poverty, the number of children in poverty is close to 50 percent. One of the biggest misunderstandings is the difference between percentages and numbers. The greatest number of children in poverty are white, but the greatest percentage of children in poverty is by minority group.

3. Generational and situational poverty are different. It generally takes two generations to make the slide from middle class into poverty. When an individual has been in poverty two generations or more, then the patterns and habits are different. Situational poverty is when there is a divorce, death, or illness, and the resources are temporarily reduced, but the mind-set remains largely with middle-class norms and values.

4. This work is based upon patterns of the group, and all patterns have exceptions.

5. Every individual brings with him or her the hidden rules of the economic group in which he or she was raised. Hidden rules are those unspoken cueing mechanisms we use to let people know they do or do not belong.

6. Schools and businesses use the hidden rules of middle class. So do many churches. Because America now tends to be economically segregated, most individuals do not know the rules of other economic classes.

7. For churches to be successful with the poor, members must understand the hidden rules of generational poverty as well as middle class, so that the transition can be more readily accepted. For the transition to occur, both sets of rules must be openly acknowledged.

8. To move from poverty to middle-class norms and values, a period of time exists where some relationships are broken. These relationships may be resumed at another time, but there is a period of time in which the old relationships are very tentative and, sometimes, broken.

9. The fundamental reasons for poverty are lack of educational attainment and the disconnection of family and/or community.

From *Nickel and Dimed: On (Not) Getting By in America* by Barbara Ehrenreich, p. 221:

> The "working poor," as they are approvingly termed, are in fact the major philanthropists of our society. They neglect their own children so that the children of others will be cared for; they live in substandard housing so that other homes will be shiny and perfect; they endure privation so that inflation will be low and stock prices high. To be a member of the working poor is to be an anonymous donor, a nameless benefactor, to everyone else.

From *The Betrayal of Work: How Low-Wage Jobs Fail 30 Million Americans* by Beth Shulman (New York: The New Press, 2003), p. 12:

> Without change, a growing gap between the haves and have-nots will continue to challenge our national solidarity and stability and will strain an already divisive America. But just as important, if work does not work for millions of Americans it undermines our country's most fundamental ideals. We are permitting a caste system to grow up around us, consigning millions of Americans to a social dead-end. The notion of equal opportunity becomes a farce in the face of these hard class divisions. It is a sentence passed onto not only those now toiling in the poverty wage economy, but onto many of their children who lack the support they need to succeed.

Learning more about Debra's congregation
Emmaus Lutheran, a first-ring suburb congregation
Description by Craig Van Gelder

This congregation was started in 1951 as new suburban housing was built on the north side of the city. Many of the tract homes were initially purchased by veterans with Veterans Administration loans. By the 1960s, this area was incorporated as a separate suburb. These young families had large numbers of children during the baby-boom years, and it seemed like the church couldn't add enough space during the 1950s and 1960s. In the first two decades, a significant number of the members of this church were made up of young families from two primary sources. Some transferred in from Lutheran city-neighborhood congregations in which they had grown up. Others transferred in from Lutheran small-town congregations throughout the state, having moved to the city.

The suburb peaked in population at 47,500 during the early 1970s as the baby-boom children left the neighborhood. During this time, the congregation also peaked in growth. A significant number of empty-nester families relocated to suburbs further out during the 1980s, but many still drive back to attend Emmaus. Two other population shifts have also been occurring in the past two decades. One is young, white couples purchasing affordable houses as starter homes but within a decade relocating to a suburb further out as their families begin to grow. Those who are Emmaus members usually transfer to a congregation nearer their new home. The other is composed of emerging middle-class Hispanic and African American families who are buying homes in the neighborhood.

Moving into action

Reflecting on your own experience

1. What are your images of "the poor"?

2. Describe your perceptions of a woman living in poverty. A male. A child. A family.

3. Reread Debra's journal. Which of the eight resources does the congregation (or individuals in the congregation) make accessible for Debra? How does that affect Debra and her family?

4. Examine your congregation for the availability and accessibility of the eight resources. Use the questions below to begin your assessment. What are the implications for mission?

Financial

Does the congregation meet its budgeted expenses?

Is the budgeting process open and transparent?

Does the congregation pay a livable wage to all staff?

Do lay staff members receive the same benefits that clergy receive?

Does the congregation give an appropriate percentage to mission support?

Does the congregation give financial support to local/community programs?

Physical

Are the church facilities handicapped accessible?

Are the facilities maintained and clean?

Are the church grounds landscaped and maintained for beauty as well as safety?

Is the church hospitable and welcoming to people of a variety of languages, cultures, economic levels (signage, artwork, and so forth)?

Mental

Do sermons, programs, and educational offerings encourage people to think about their faith and life?

Are members and staff encouraged to learn and grow?

Are sermons accessible for people of all ages, classes, and cultures?

Emotional

Does the congregation exhibit emotional health and integrity?

Are decisions made in an equitable and fair manner?

Are tough issues discussed openly?

Are disagreements handled respectfully?

Is pastoral counseling available?

Spiritual

Do clergy and lay leaders exhibit faithful living?

Do worship and the programs of the congregation encourage members to grow in their faith?

Are there in-depth opportunities for people to learn and grow in their discipleship?

Would people without a Christian faith tradition be introduced to and nurtured in their faith?

Support systems

Are children and youth nurtured and mentored in a safe faith environment?

Is there a discretionary fund to aid in emergencies?

Are there programs that support people or educational programs for ESL, job training, citizenship training, and so forth?

Is childcare available?

Is the congregation involved in Stephen Ministry (or similar ministry of support)?

Relationships/role models

Are mentoring relationships available (formally or informally) for children, youth, and adults?

Are cross-cultural relationships evident among members and visitors?

Are friendships and caring relationships easy to establish and maintain?

Knowledge of the hidden rules

Is worship accessible for children and for visitors?

Do members readily greet and guide newcomers in worship and assimilation into the congregation?

Are mental models/basic assumptions that guide the life of the congregation articulated and communicated and critiqued?

5. Use the questions below to examine your community for the accessibility of the eight resources. What are the implications for your congregation's mission and for community involvement?

Financial
Are there living-wage jobs available in the community?
Are there banks and credit unions?
Is affordable housing available?

Physical
Is quality health care available?
Is the crime rate low?
Are there parks, sidewalks, bike trails, and so forth?
Is there a variety of safe housing?

Mental
Are good public schools and libraries available?
What is the graduation rate? The drop-out rate?
What are the test scores in math and reading?

Emotional
Are community policy decisions made which enhance the well-being of the residents?
Is the community safe, productive, and predictable?

Spiritual
Are the congregations in the community healthy and viable?
Are they welcoming to all of the people in the community?
Are they involved and invested in the community?

Support systems
Is there an active neighborhood association?
Is quality childcare available and affordable?

Are police and fire departments available?

Is transportation or a transit system accessible and effective?

Relationships/role models

Are there supportive family systems in the community?

Are there other mentoring or partnering relationships available?

Knowledge of the hidden rules

Is there healthy interaction between people of differing economic classes and cultural backgrounds?

Do there seem to be friendships and mutual respect among people of diverse backgrounds?

Personal action plan

1. Think about your own life and your own situation. Which of the eight resources are available and accessible to you? Which ones are your strengths? Which resources need strengthening? How might you work from your strengths to improve the other resources?

2. Do you know someone in a similar situation as Debra (male or female)? If so, which of your strengths could enhance his or her accessibility to the eight resources? If you do not know someone in Debra's similar situation, ask your pastor or a school teacher or social service agency about other "Debras." Listen to her (or his) story. Remember that not all people who live in poverty are single parents or female.

3. Volunteer to help serve a meal at a shelter (family or singles shelter). While there, visit with at least one person and hear his or her story.

4. Read one or parts of several of the references listed in the section on "Resources" and the quotes in "Perspectives." Identify any new ideas or insights you may have discovered.

Group activities

1. Discuss the working definition of poverty as "the extent to which an individual does without resources." Do you think this is a helpful and accurate definition?

2. Discuss the difference between generational poverty and situational poverty. Have you ever experienced either generational or situational poverty?

3. Reread Debra's story and her journal. Compare your thoughts about which of the resources were available—or became available—to her and her family. Discuss the implications for the mission of your congregation.

4. Discuss your assessments of your congregation's and your community's resources. Discuss the implications for mission. Identify your congregation's and community's strengths. How can you use the strengths to enhance the availability of all of the resources? Begin to develop a plan.

5. Name at least one action that you will do, together or individually, as a result of this discussion and planning. Agree to hold one another mutually accountable for that action.

2

Communities of Poverty

Jack's story

Jack hadn't always told his friends this, but he had first wondered if God might be calling him to be a pastor when he was in high school. It all began when his youth group went to Atlanta to a national youth gathering and had stayed to work in a small multicultural congregation led by a lively African American ELCA pastor and her musician husband. Their commitment to the people and issues of their community had made an impact on Jack, and he came back with two new insights: (1) He knew God was calling him to work in some kind of urban ministry, and (2) he was so grateful that he lived and worked in the Twin Cities, where the urban issues were so different than in the South and in places like Atlanta. He was glad that his "Cities" were more progressive in race relations and their treatment of the poor than in some other parts of the country. Because of his interest in urban issues, he chose to attend a college located in the city, and to major in political science.

Now, here he was—a student in seminary and doing his internship in an urban congregation in Saint Paul. What a perfect internship site for his gifts and interests and passions! But the more he talked with his supervising pastor and got to know the congregation and the community, the more something began to haunt him. He had always been so proud of his "Cities" and saw them as superior to other cities. Now he was hearing some disturbing stories from the people in the community and observing some confusing signs. He was trying to make sense of it.

Why was it that people who were poor seemed to live in particular neighborhoods of the metropolitan area, primarily in the central areas of the city? How did that come about and what sustained that phenomenon?

Why was it that so many living in poverty actually held full-time jobs but still seemed to be trapped in poverty?

Why did more people of color live in the communities of poverty than in other parts of the metropolitan area? Was that a matter of choice or was something else going on?

Why was unemployment higher in these areas than in the outer suburbs?

Why was the crime rate higher?

Why did businesses and schools in the areas of poverty seem different from the schools in other areas—such as in the neighborhood in which he had grown up?

How could it be that he had lived in the Cities all of his life and had not noticed or asked these questions before? Had Saint Paul and Minneapolis changed, or had he—or both?

What were the factors that changed a neighborhood, like the one around his internship church, from a thriving middle class community into an area of concentrated poverty?

And why were there so few from the neighborhood—Hispanics, African Americans, Asians, and American Indians—who were members of his internship congregation?

He could sense these were important questions with no easy, or comforting, answers, but he also suspected they were questions that had implications for the congregation's mission. What was God leading them to do in this time and in this place?

Jack's journal
Monday

Dear God, what a day! It was supposed to be my day off, but I spent it at the hospital. Poor little Gracie, hanging on to her nine-year-old life with all she's got. She and her eight-year-old brother Ramón live with their grandmother near the church, and they were playing on the front porch, innocently playing with Ramón's new Game Boy—a gift from their mostly-absent father. Two small children playing on their grandmother's front porch ought to be safe! But they weren't!

The police think the shooting was gang-related and the bullet that pierced Gracie's lung was meant for one of the rival gang members on the street. But whether or not it was a stray bullet and not meant for Gracie, she's still critically injured.

And, oh, the suffering of her grandmother, who feels so responsible for her daughter's two children—and who loves Gracie and Ramón dearly. Today was really the first time I met Mrs. Alvarez. She had allowed Gracie and Ramón to come to our after-school program at the church. So when the hospital staff asked her if they should call someone from her faith community, the only church she knew was ours. We couldn't talk much because her English is on the same par as my Spanish, but she seemed to appreciate my presence.

This has been one of those really heartbreaking but mountain-top days. God, be with Gracie—and Ramón and Mrs. Alvarez.

Tuesday

I went back to the hospital this afternoon and Gracie is responding a bit. The surgery was seemingly successful but she is still in critical condition. I did get to go into ICU briefly and pray by her bedside with Mrs. A. Gracie looks so fragile. Please, God, be with them.

Today Juan (Gracie and Ramón's father) was there also. Actually, he is their stepfather and is a U. S. citizen. Their mother was deported back to Mexico when Immigration found her papers were not up to date. They've now been trying to get her an emergency visa so she can come to be with Gracie.

Juan has a full-time job but it's located in an outlying suburb and, without a car, he has to rely on a friend and coworker for transportation. That's why he bunks out in a back room at his friend's house. I'm not sure everything Juan told me is completely accurate—I noticed some tension between Mrs. A. and Juan—but it was clear he loves Gracie and Ramón and is full of hatred toward the person who shot Gracie. Now that I think about it, that may be the source of the tension I saw. I wonder if Mrs. A. is afraid that Juan will try to get revenge if he finds out who did this and then he will get caught, go to prison, and the children will be without both parents. That would mean she would have all of the responsibility for them, and she knows her wages from her job at the day care cannot pay the rent, buy food and clothing for Gracie and Ramón, and cover all the other day-to-day expenses. And that doesn't even take Gracie's mounting hospital bills into account. I wonder what their insurance situation is. (No one has said—and I haven't asked—anything about Gracie and Ramón's birth father, but I gather that he is nowhere in the picture anymore.)

Oh, how sad and complex life is for people like Mrs. A. and Juan and little Gracie and Ramón. And our congregation is located in the midst of people with similar stories. God, what are you calling us to do?

Wednesday

When I arrived at church this morning, I met Reggie walking on the sidewalk. I hadn't seen him in a while, and he seemed more confused than usual. I asked him where he was staying, and he pointed and gave a vague answer. He was able to give me the name of his county case worker, so I called and asked if Reggie is on his meds. She said she thought so, but when someone is on the street there is no way to be certain.

I had told Reggie to wait while I made a phone call, but by the time I got off the phone, he had already left the building. I feel so helpless. Carl, my supervisor, told me once that Reggie had been in the army and had served in Vietnam. Something just doesn't seem right; after serving his country, now he lives on the streets, or in a shelter if he's lucky. I've heard there are many "Reggies" among the homeless.

I called to check on Gracie, and the nurse was willing to tell me she's improving. I also heard on the news that the police have identified and caught two suspects. I wonder what Juan will do. Tomorrow I'm going to try to have a conversation with him.

Thursday

Okay, God, some things are becoming disturbingly clear and it's all tying right back to my sense of call. I've been ranting and raving to Carl about the inequities in this community—the lack of living-wage jobs, transportation, good housing; the unfair immigration laws; the gangs; etc. Carl said he's been so concerned about keeping the congregation alive that he hasn't been able to think "outside the box." He said he knew the congregation needed to be part of the solutions in the community and reach out to the people more. He also thought that the congregation had at one time, before his time, looked into joining the faith-based community organizing effort, but, for some reason, they had not joined. We both think it would be good for me to talk with some of the congregation members who are interested in the mission of the church in this community and in the public arena, and perhaps we can together discover more about what we should do. Carl also suggested that I might want to do some further demographic research about this area.

This afternoon I went to the hospital and found out that Gracie was moved out of ICU. In my very poor Spanish, I asked Mrs. A. where Juan worked and she told me. She also asked me to pray for Rosa, her daughter—that she will be allowed to come. I told her I would.

I drove out to Juan's job—on a hotel maintenance crew—and caught him right as he was starting the night shift. He had heard that the police have two suspects and his anger was quite evident. I hope he doesn't explode at work and lose his job. He did say he wasn't going to do anything crazy, but he may have been saying that for my benefit. I asked him if I could call him tomorrow at work and he said he could take a call on his evening lunch break.

Friday

I took off most of the day (since I missed my regular day off on Monday), but I did call Juan this evening on his break. He doesn't think Rosa is going to get the emergency visa, but he did say that Gracie is continuing to improve. He said he would like to move the whole family closer to his job—which pays fairly well—but there's no way he can afford even an apartment anywhere near his work. He says he feels caught—(1) there aren't any jobs in the neighborhood around where he and Rosa and the kids live with Mrs. A., (2) there's no housing he can afford near his work, and (3) there aren't any buses that go anywhere near his job. What a catch-22 situation! So his only hope is to get a car soon, so he can make it back and forth each day from Mrs. A's house to his job.

He didn't mention the two suspects, and it didn't seem appropriate to ask him about it over the phone, especially when he started talking about his other very real concerns. He did seem interested in staying in contact.

Saturday

Gracie actually opened her eyes and smiled when I visited her today. Ramón was there with Mrs. A., and he and I sang some of the songs from our after-school program for her. She is very weak but she is quite a fighter. I saw Mrs. A. smile for the first time this week. I think I am developing a relationship with this struggling but resilient family.

Later I called up some of the congregation members that Carl and I think may have an interest in the congregation's public ministry—and have a passion for helping the community. Six of them were interested in having lunch together tomorrow after worship. Both Carl and I will be there. I'm to bring some of the demographic information about our congregation and our area, so we can look at it together.

God, I wonder if this congregation could have the leadership needed to make a difference in this community. If so, we need to strengthen the congregation, understand what turned this community into a community of concentrated poverty, and join with other congregations to work for racial and economic justice and health for families like Juan and Mrs. A. and for individuals like Reggie.

Going deeper
Communities of concentrated poverty

Every community—rural, suburban, or urban—consists of various threads interwoven to create a community and its identity and characteristics. The threads of businesses, schools, congregations, government, agencies, and so forth, crisscross with the variety of people and cultures. People who are economically poor can live in economically diverse communities in any part of a city, suburb, or rural area. For this study, we will focus on the aspects that cause and perpetuate communities of concentrated poverty—communities in which more than 40 percent of the population earns less than federal poverty guidelines (in 2005, $9,570 for a single person, $19,350 for a family of four). For further statistics on poverty in the United States, see the U.S. Census Bureau Web site: www.census.gov/hhes/www/poverty.html.

Within most U.S. metropolitan areas can be found one or more communities of concentrated poverty. This area is usually located in or near the central city, with some recent (1990s) disbursement outward into the first-ring suburbs.

To understand and address poverty, we need to examine the major characteristics of these communities of concentrated poverty, identify the factors that created them, and meet and know the people living in these communities.

In the opening narrative, Jack was beginning to ask the tough questions—questions that may disturb us but also questions that are necessary if we will indeed work to eliminate poverty. Under the leadership of Myron Orfield, executive director of the Metropolitan Area Research Corporation and a Minnesota state senator, data has been organized into useful maps that show various characteristics of twenty-five major metropolitan areas in the United States. The maps are available at www.ameregis.com. Click on "Reports & Maps."

One particular set of maps, "Percentage of Elementary Students Eligible for Free Lunch by School, 1997," clearly shows that in each of the twenty-five urban areas the community of concentrated poverty is located in the central city.

All of the eight resources (see chapter 1, page 35) need to be available in a community—resources such as living wage jobs, affordable housing, health care, healthy and high-performing schools, thriving congregations, and effective transit systems. When these resources are in trouble, the whole community suffers. These areas need addressing in order to end poverty.

In his study titled "Stunning Progress, Hidden Problems: The Dramatic Decline of Concentrated Poverty in the 1990s (2003)," Professor of Political Economy Paul A. Jargowsky (2003) reveals that some changes occurred in high-poverty neighborhoods in the decade of the 1990s. A summary of his findings indicates the following:

- The number of people living in high-poverty neighborhoods— where the poverty rate is 40 percent or higher—declined by a dramatic 24 percent, or 2.5 million people, in the 1990s.
- The steepest declines in high-poverty neighborhoods occurred in metropolitan areas in the Midwest and South.

- Concentrated poverty—the share of the poor living in high-poverty neighborhoods—declined among all racial and ethnic groups, especially African Americans.
- The number of high-poverty neighborhoods declined in rural areas and central cities, but suburbs experienced almost no change. A number of older, inner-ring suburbs around major metropolitan areas actually experienced increases in poverty over the decade.

However, he continues that, "while the 1990s brought a landmark reversal of decades of increasingly concentrated poverty, the recent economic downturn and the weakening state of many older suburbs underscore that the trend may reverse once again without continued efforts to promote economic and residential opportunity for low-income families" (The Brookings Institution Web site: www.brookings.edu/es/urban/publications/jargowskypoverty.htm).

Connection between poverty and race

Integrally interwoven with all of the resources of a community is the aspect of race and ethnicity. To draw a connection between poverty and race is fraught with the possibility of misunderstanding and misperception. However, the following graph may help clarify.

In the 2000 census, the following ethnic percentages and numbers of poor children were reported.

United States	Number of children in poverty in 1999	Percent of children in poverty
All races	12,109,000	16.9
White	7,568,000	13.5
African American	3,759,000	33.1
Hispanic*	3,506,000	30.3
Asian American	361,000	11.8
Native American+	260,403	39.8

Source: U.S. Bureau of the Census; *Hispanics may be of any race.
+Native American numbers from 1990 (not counted in 1999).

Notice that the numbers and percentages represent those children living in poverty in the United States in 1999. The graph shows that in raw numbers there are more white children living in poverty (12,109,000) than any other race. However, in examining the percentages, the largest percentage of children living in poverty are American Indians (39.8 percent), followed by African Americans (33.1 percent) and Hispanics (30.3 percent). These statistics do not imply that all persons of that race or ethnicity are poor, but they do show a disturbingly high ratio of children of color who live in poverty—primarily in areas of concentrated poverty.

When two of the maps developed by Myron Orfield and Ameregis (a research and geographic information systems firm), "Percentage of Elementary Students Eligible for Free Lunch by School, 1997" and "Percentage of Non-Asian Minority Elementary Students by School, 1997," are viewed side-by-side, a compelling correlation between them can be seen. These two maps show us that a high percentage of children living in poverty are children of color.

The findings of john a. powell (lowercase is correct), as reported in *Racism and Metropolitan Dynamics: The Civil Rights Challenge of the 21st Century*, give further sobering evidence of racial disparities in the United States as a whole (Minneapolis: Institute on Race and Poverty, 2002, 6-7).

- African Americans and Latinos have poverty rates nearly three times as high as those of whites.
- People of color are disproportionately represented in neighborhoods in which 40 percent or more of residents live in poverty—"concentrated poverty" is racialized.
- African American and Latino students obtain college degrees at half the rate of white students.
- For roughly the past twenty years, the unemployment rate for African Americans has been twice that for whites.
- More than fourteen million jobs were created in the nation between 1993 and 1998, but only 13 percent of these jobs were

in central cities. Looking at entry-level jobs specifically in 1999, researchers found that predominantly white suburbs host nearly 70 percent of these jobs while central cities lost merely 10 percent. Low-income people of color who cannot find affordable housing in the suburbs or who must use limited public transportation are effectively blocked from employment opportunities in distant suburbs. The spatial arrangement (or mismatch) of the labor pool and jobs contributes to employment disparities by race.

If it is true that the areas of concentrated poverty are populated disproportionately by people of color, we cannot avoid or ignore the same tough questions Jack asked.

- What is the connection between poverty and race in the United States in general and in our own urban area in particular?
- Can we effectively work to end poverty without also working to end discriminatory structures, systems, and policies that keep people, many of whom are people of color, in poverty?

Even a cursory reading of Ronald Takaki's *A Different Mirror: A History of Multicultural America* (Boston: Little, Brown and Company, 1993) reveals that the United States was formed as a "racialized" society. Laws, policies, governmental, and even ecclesial structures were racially-based and, therefore, racially-biased. As a result, the whole fabric of society suffers.

Now God calls us to work together to build a just and equitable community that enhances and blesses the central city, the suburbs, and the rural areas alike. It is a call worthy of our passion and commitment.

Bible study

Read Exodus 3:7-12. The Israelites were living in an area of concentrated poverty and oppression. They were not paid a livable wage and their oppression was clearly based on their race.

What was God's attitude toward the Israelites?

For what purpose was God calling Moses?
How does this story connect to God's call today?

Read Isaiah 24:1-13. Describe this "city of chaos."
What, in your opinion, are the similarities with and differences from your metropolitan area?

Read Deuteronomy 15:1-11 (especially verse 11) and Matthew 26:6-13 (especially verse 11). How do these passages "fit" together?
How does the passage from Deuteronomy shed light on Jesus' statement in Matthew 26?

Read Luke 10:25-37 and John 4:1-30. Samaritans were a mixed race and, in Jesus' day, considered "less than."
What do these texts reveal about Jesus' stance toward Samaritans?

Resources

American Research and Geographic Information Systems Web site: www.ameregis.com

ELCA Congregation Trend Report, Department for Research and Evaluation, Evangelical Lutheran Church in America Web site: www.elca.org/re/trendnet.html

Maeker, Nancy. "Whom Shall I Send and Who Will Go for Us? Identifying Persons with Potential for Cross-Cultural Mission," Chapter 2. DMin. thesis, Luther Seminary, 1998.

Orfield, Myron. *Metropolitics: A Regional Agenda for Community and Stability.* Rev. ed. Washington, D.C.: Brookings Institution Press, 1998.

Orfield, Myron. *American Metropolitics: The New Suburban Reality.* Washington, D.C., Brookings Institution Press, 2002.

powell, john a. *Racism and Metropolitan Dynamics: The Civil Rights Challenge of the 21st Century.* Minneapolis: Institute on Race and Poverty, 2002.

"Stunning Progress, Hidden Problems: The Dramatic Decline of Concentrated Poverty in the 1990s." The Brookings Institution: www.brookings.edu/es/urban/publications/jargowskypoverty.htm

Suskind, Ron. *A Hope in the Unseen: An American Odyssey from the Inner City to the Ivy League*. New York: Broadway Books, 1998.

Takaki, Ronald. *A Different Mirror: A History of Multicultural America*. Boston: Little, Brown and Company, 1993.

Wallis, Jim. *God's Politics: Why the Right Gets It Wrong and the Left Doesn't Get It*. San Francisco: HarperSanFrancisco, 2005.

Perspectives

From "How the government set the stage for today's structural racial injustices" by john a. powell in *Racism and Metropolitan Dynamics: The Civil Rights Challenge of the 21st Century*, pp. 9-10:

The departure of Whites from the central city was no accident, nor was the isolation of people of color in central cities that now are fraught with a multitude of problems. The federal government played a central role. As Kenneth Jackson and others have described, the government first opened up the suburbs to Whites via the National Housing Act of 1934. This law created the Home Ownership Loan Corporation, which subsidized home mortgages for Whites in the suburbs, a practice continued later by the Federal Housing Administration. . . .

The government explicitly offered these subsidies to Whites, would only fund houses in racially homogeneous, White neighborhoods, and favored the purchase of homes in the suburbs. The underwriting manual for home mortgage insurance disseminated by the federal government was explicitly racist:

Areas surrounding a location are (to be) investigated to determine whether incompatible racial and social groups are present, for the purpose of making a prediction regarding the probability of the location being invaded by such groups.

If a neighborhood is to retain stability, it is necessary that properties shall continue to be occupied by the same social and racial classes.

Furthermore, the federal government pushed home purchasers to adopt covenants that prohibited the future sale of these government-subsidized homes to people of color. . . .

The opening of the suburbs to Whites also was subsidized by the government through the creation and funding of highways. By the Federal Aid Highway Act of 1956, the federal government became the largest funder of the interstate highway system. These highways were intended for long-distance travel, but over half of the funding had gone to highways within metropolitan regions as of the mid-1990s, according to David Rusk and others. In other words, the federal government bankrolled Whites' departure and created easy access to jobs and other institutions within regions for suburban residents over a span of decades. . . .

Kenneth Jackson revealed that highway spending has eclipsed transit spending by a 5-to-1 margin during the past half-dozen decades.

From Mary Lethert Wingerd's *Claiming the City: Politics, Faith, and the Power of Place in St. Paul* (Ithaca: Cornell University Press, 2001), pp. 77, 79-81, 83-84:

The racial fluidity of frontier St. Paul had been of short duration. In fact, by the mid-1850s, St. Paul legislators had attempted first to pass a bill discouraging black in-migration and, when that failed, a measure that would restrict black residency to Minneapolis—hardly gestures of either interracial or intercity fraternity. . . .

Then there was "invisible" St. Paul, the pockets of poverty that had no place in the emerging civic vision. Hidden away from the public gaze, the city's poor could count on little support from official sources. Those who populated "Little Italy" on the river flats on the east bank of the river, the eastern Europeans who claimed the flats on the western side, the down-and-out Irishmen who battled Swedes and Italians for scarce resources in "Swede Hollow," a deep ravine below Hamm's Brewery on the East Side, or the mixed population of Connemara Patch, stashed away amidst the tracks and trestles of lower Payne Avenue—all were left largely to find their own means of survival.

Though they provided an essential source of unskilled labor, these city residents received no commensurate share of public resources in return. In Swede Hollow, for example, a ramshackle cluster of jerry-built houses, the city never saw fit to extend either running water or sewers to its residents, though for more than seventy years it housed a succession of immigrant workers—Swedes, Italians, Poles, and, finally, Mexicans. . . .

The physical terrain of the city also acted to maintain the invisibility of its poor. . . . All were spatially as well as culturally disconnected from the city proper. . . . Workers emerged from these neighborhoods every morning to dig the ditches, stoke the fires, and wash the clothes of their fellow St. Paulites but were quickly forgotten when they disappeared at the end of the day. In working out the complicated negotiations and compromises that underlay St. Paul's civic relationships, the city's poor were truly out of sight and most definitely out of mind.

Learning more about Jack's internship congregation
Second Lutheran, a city-neighborhood congregation
Description by Craig Van Gelder

New immigrants entering the city started this congregation in the first decade of the twentieth century. Most of the membership was made up of working-class families who had not felt at home attending First Church and who desired to have a church that was in their immediate neighborhood. This neighborhood was located just north of the original downtown area. When the church began, all services were held in the native Scandinavian language, and this continued well into the 1930s. When the church was started, a streetcar line ran past its location one block to the west. Because the original members either walked to church or took the streetcar, no off-street parking was ever acquired.

Following World War II, significant changes took place in the old neighborhood as young families moved to the suburbs and much of the original housing was torn down in an urban renewal project related to the interstate highway. In recent decades, further changes have come with communities of Hmong and Hispanic persons moving into the area. Second Lutheran's membership is still predominantly white and is mostly made up of older adult persons who share a Scandinavian heritage, but the majority of these remaining members no longer live in the immediate neighborhood. Those who now attend often find it difficult to find sufficient parking within a reasonable walking distance on nearby streets.

Moving into action
Reflecting on your own experience

1. Explore some of the Web sites listed in this chapter, paying particular attention to the area in which you live. As you do, jot down your questions or comments to discuss with others.
2. Read one or parts of several of the books listed in this chapter.
3. Does any of the material presented in this chapter disturb you? If so, make a list of your concerns and reflect on them and discuss them with others; do further research on those topics. Does your place of residence affect your response in any way? Can you identify the reasons?

4. Reread Jack's journal. Which of the eight resources are available and which are in trouble in the community around Second Lutheran? What do you think Jack's internship congregation will do?

Personal action plan

1. Read the excerpts from *Claiming the City* by Mary Lehnert Wingerd. Does your community or urban area have historic ethnic enclaves such as the ones named in Saint Paul? Identify the characteristics that you know about each community. You may need to visit those areas and do some demographic research to find out accurate and current information about these areas. How have these communities changed over the past 50 years?
2. This chapter has focused on communities of concentrated poverty, especially in the central city and first-ring suburbs. Determine whether there are "pockets of poverty" in or near your home community—rural, suburban, or urban. Discover who the residents are and what some of the causes of poverty might be.
3. Find out if your congregation has been involved in acts of service, advocacy, or other organizing efforts working toward just and equitable communities.
4. Determine a plan of action based on this chapter. Discuss it with trusted congregation members and, if you choose, invite them to participate in the plan. Ask someone to hold you accountable.

Getting together with others

1. Invite someone to speak to congregation members whose congregation is active in a synodical or faith-based community organizing effort. Discuss how their faith connects to their involvement. Discuss whether congregational planning and working together can bring about healthy change in your particular area.
2. If you had questions, comments, or concerns from "Reflecting on Your Own Experience," discuss those questions and concerns with the group.

3. Discuss "A Common Foundation: Shared Principles for Work on Overcoming Poverty" on page 13, written by Bishop Peter Rogness, and signed by thirty-four religious leaders in Minnesota. What would your community, state, nation look like if these principles became reality?

4. Read the appendix, "Ending Poverty: A Biblical Moral Mandate within Civil Society," on page 97 to learn about one model for living out "A Common Foundation."

3

The Hidden Culture of Class

Harold's story

To say Harold was frustrated as he left work was a gross under-statement. He had thought he was doing the right thing, even the Christian thing—in fact he had told his wife, Betty, that he felt something like a "call" to run the company this way. But now he just didn't know at all.

Harold is the owner of a small manufacturing company and he employs twenty to twenty-five workers, depending on seasonal demand and the workers he can find for some of the less skilled jobs.

His "sense of call"—and his troubles—all began when he decided to take seriously some of the discussions in the discipleship classes at church as well as some sermons he had heard.

So he decided to change the "bottom-line" thinking that people in business usually assume. He decided that he would raise the pay scale for the lower skilled positions, provide full benefits, and hire people who came out of poverty. That way he might be doing his part to provide living-wage jobs for several people and raise the income level for those families. In essence he was trying his own mini-experiment—to see if doing the right thing for people could also become the right thing for business. Betty supported him in his plan.

Well, he had hired two men, Ralph and George, who had both grown up in poverty and were still not really any better off than their parents had been. They both seemed so eager and grateful for their jobs, but it just wasn't working out. First they didn't always get to work on time. If they're so grateful for the job, reasoned Harold, the least they could do is get there on time!

Then there was the way they spoke to the other workers. Several of the long-time women employees had complained to him about their inappropriate language. But the worst part was that he couldn't seem to get them to understand what they were doing wrong. And today when he tried to tell them how they needed to change, Ralph got all huffy and left work, and George shouted obscenities at him and stormed out of the room.

Was he going to have to give up and fire them both?

Harold's journal

Monday

Betty was helpful when I told her how frustrated I was with Ralph and George and how I was ready to fire them both. She reminded me why I had decided to do this in the first place. I really did think it was the right thing to do—and maybe I still do—but that doesn't mean it's easy. I'll see if they show up for work tomorrow.

Tuesday

Today it was like nothing ever happened . . . so I sort of avoided Ralph and George and tended to other business. But I know I can't ignore some of the issues altogether. Janice, my administrative assistant, keeps raising her eyebrows every time I walk past her, like she's asking, "Well, when are you going to deal with them?"

Tonight Betty pulled out a book from my stack on the bedside table and asked if I had read it. The book is the one I bought at church after an adult forum on ending poverty. That forum was part of my reason for hiring Ralph and George in the first place. I had to admit that I hadn't even opened the book. I thought I knew more than any author about how to work with employees, and I surely didn't think the church could provide any resources that would help make my business run better. But, now, maybe I will take a look and see what it says. Here it is—*Hidden Rules of Class at Work* by Ruby Payne and Don Krabill . . . hmm, we'll see.

Wednesday

Well, last night I didn't get very far in the book because I was so tired, but I think it might be helpful. If Ralph and George are coming out of generational poverty and my other employees and I are from the middle class, then we are experiencing something like a clashing of cultures. That puts things in a different light. Maybe I won't fire Ralph and George until I find out more about this whole situation.

Thursday

I brought the book with me to work today and suggested to Janice that she take a longer lunch break and read parts of it. When she came back she gave the book back with a smile and a nod. I think she is seeing the same potential for understanding that I am. We'll have to find time to discuss this further. I also remembered that there were several other business people who attended the same adult forum that I did. I wonder if any of them also tried something new after that. I may call Hugh tomorrow.

Friday

I did call Hugh today. He said he hadn't done anything different after the adult forum, but he was interested in hearing about my situation. He also said that he had bought and actually read the same book and was thinking how it might explain some conflicts among his employees. Anyway, he suggested that we meet for lunch next week and discuss this matter.

Saturday

I decided to finish reading the book today and found it shed a lot of light on my situation at work. Hidden rules can be pretty powerful, and we don't even realize how much they are controlling us and our work places. This is really interesting stuff. I think I may even discuss this with several people tomorrow at church and maybe even get a group of business people together. This may be one of those "calls" after all.

Going deeper
The hidden rules of class

R. D. Laing, a noted philosopher and psychologist, once wrote this circular saying:

> The range of what we think and do
> Is limited by what we fail to notice.
> And because we fail to notice
> That we fail to notice
> There is little we can do
> To change
> Until we notice
> How failing to notice
> Shapes our thoughts and deeds.
> (As quoted on ThinkExist.com)

In a way Laing was describing culture—all of those unspoken, hidden rules that make up the way of life of a people. We often think of culture as relating only to our racial or ethnic backgrounds—the traditional foods, the music, the humor, the manner of speaking and relating, for example. But the term "culture" can also explain the differences in economic class.

What Harold and the several long-time employees were confronting was the difference in economic cultures. George and Ralph both came out of generational poverty and operated out of the hidden rules of their culture. Harold came out of a middle-class culture, and, although he had a strong desire and commitment to "help" those in poverty, the hidden rules of his class culture were getting in his way.

In fact, all businesses, schools, institutions, and congregations exhibit their own culture—the hidden way of life of a people. In most cases in academic and business worlds, the culture is that of middle class. That means that anyone from generational poverty who enters into one of those cultural settings will have a difficult time fitting in because of cultural differences. Therefore, the cultural differences need to be identified, named, discussed, and made known to people in poverty and middle class (and wealth) if any bridges will be built across these economic cultural divides.

Congregations and whole denominations exhibit characteristics of one economic class or another. I doubt if many would argue with the suggestion that the Evangelical Lutheran Church in America and most of its congregations exhibit middle-class patterns, behaviors, and values. Our present challenge and our opportunity may now be to "notice how failing to notice shapes our thoughts and deeds," as R. D. Laing wrote.

The need to name cultural ways of being is a necessary step, for a congregation or an entire denomination, in reaching out and inviting people of a culture other than the dominant culture. So what then is our mission call?

Bible study

Read Acts 10:1-48. Peter and Cornelius came from different cultural—ethnic, economic, and religious—backgrounds.

Identify some of the mental models (basic assumptions) that each had about the other.

How did Peter's assumptions change after he had been in Cornelius's home and had eaten with his family?

Read Ephesians 2:11-22. This passage refers to the differences and distinctions between Jews and Gentiles and affirms that Christ "has broken down the dividing wall, that is, the hostility between us . . . that he might create in himself one new humanity in place of the two, thus making peace, and might reconcile both groups to God in one body through the cross, thus putting to death that hostility through it" (vv. 14-16).

Reflect on any dividing walls you have noticed at work or in your congregation.

How does this passage apply?

Read Luke 14:7-24. Reflect on the various economic cultural references in these teachings of Jesus.

How did Jesus relate to people of various economic classes?

What does it mean for you?

Read Luke 10:29-37. What were the mental models that the priest, the Levite, and the Samaritan were operating out of?

How did their mental models determine their actions?

Resources

Maeker, Nancy. *Cross-cultural Evangelism: Helping Congregations Reach Out*, Session 3. Minneapolis: Augsburg Fortress, 1993.

Payne, Ruby K., Ph.D. and Don L. Krabill. *Hidden Rules of Class at Work*. Highlands, Texas: aha! Process, Inc., 2002.

Payne, Ruby K., and Bill Ehlig. *What Every Church Member Should Know about Poverty*. Highlands, Texas: aha! Process, Inc., 1999.

People Like Us: Social Class in America, video, Public Broadcasting Service. Information available at www.pbs.org/peoplelikeus/about/top.html

Senge, Peter M. *The Fifth Discipline: The Art and Practice of the Learning Organization*, chapter 10. New York: Doubleday, 1990.

Perspectives

From *The Fifth Discipline: The Art and Practice of the Learning Organization* by Peter Senge, pp. 175, 176, 186-187:

> Mental models can be simple generalizations such as "people are untrustworthy," or they can be complex theories, such as my assumptions about why members of my family interact as they do. But what is most important to grasp is that mental models are *active*—they shape how we act. If we believe people are untrustworthy, we act differently from the way we would if we believed they were trustworthy. If I believe that my son lacks self-confidence and my daughter is highly aggressive, I will continually intervene in their exchanges to prevent her from damaging his ego. Why are mental models so powerful in affecting what we do? In part, because they affect what we see. Two people with different mental models can observe the same event and describe it differently because they've looked at different details . . . The problems with mental models lie not in whether they are right or wrong—by definition, all models are simplifications. The problems with mental models arise when the models are tacit—when they exist below the level of awareness. . . . [The critical task, then, is] to bring key assumptions about important . . . issues to the surface. This goal . . . is vital . . . because the most crucial mental models in any organization are those shared by key decision makers. Those models, if unexamined, limit an organization's range of actions to what is familiar and comfortable."

Learning more about Harold's congregation
Christ the King Lutheran, a third-ring suburb congregation
Description by Craig Van Gelder

This mission development congregation was started in 1980 by the denomination in a growing suburban community on the far north edge of the metropolitan area. Both the community and the congregation have experienced rapid growth, with the congregation having a membership of four thousand and worshiping more than fifteen hundred in three services. The community was incorporated in the mid-1980s and has continued to experience rapid growth. Vacant farmland spaced between the various housing subdivisions is still available for building. Christ the King's mission is to reach any and all persons in this new community.

The congregation has been moderately successful in attracting formerly inactive persons from a variety of denominational backgrounds, but the majority of members are transfers from Lutheran congregations throughout the metropolitan area, the state, and the country. Christ the King wears its Lutheran identity a little more lightly than many of the other congregations in the synod. Its worship style is contemporary, its ministry is staff-led, and its senior pastor is a charismatic leader who has been with the church from its inception. The congregation is known for its excellence in programming, especially its children, youth, and family programs. In the past decade, the church has begun to sponsor a yearly conference for pastors and church leaders from other congregations to come and learn from Christ the King's experience.

Moving into action

Reflecting on your own experience

1. Can you identify some of your family's hidden rules? Name some of the unspoken rules you assume others also know and understand.
2. Think about your congregation and its mental models (see Peter Senge's quote on page 75). Name at least five mental models operating in your congregation—hidden rules that shape the way things are done. Remember that mental models are neither right nor wrong; they just are. They are assumptions that are often unconscious, agreed-upon ways of doing things.
3. Ruby Payne has developed an exercise to determine the economic class in which an individual feels most comfortable (in other words, understands the hidden rules, the unspoken cues and habits).

Take the little quiz on the next page and see some of the differences in hidden rules among the three economic classes.

A little quiz by Ruby Payne
COULD YOU SURVIVE IN POVERTY?

Put a check by each item you know how to do.

- ❏ 1. I know which churches and sections of town have the best rummage sales.
- ❏ 2. I know which rummage sales have "bag sales" and when.
- ❏ 3. I know which grocery stores' garbage bins can be accessed for thrown-away food.
- ❏ 4. I know how to get someone out of jail.
- ❏ 5. I know how to physically fight and defend myself physically.
- ❏ 6. I know how to get a gun even if I have a police record.
- ❏ 7. I know how to keep my clothes from being stolen at the laundromat.
- ❏ 8. I know what problems to look for in a used car.
- ❏ 9. I know how to live without a checking account.
- ❏ 10. I know how to live without electricity and a phone.
- ❏ 11. I know how to use a knife as scissors.
- ❏ 12. I can entertain a group of friends with my personality and my stories.
- ❏ 13. I know what to do when I don't have money to pay the bills.
- ❏ 14. I know how to move in half a day.
- ❏ 15. I know how to get and use food stamps or an electronic card for benefits.
- ❏ 16. I know where the free medical clinics are.
- ❏ 17. I am very good at trading and bartering.
- ❏ 18. I can get by without a car.

COULD YOU SURVIVE IN MIDDLE CLASS?

Put a check by each item you know how to do.

- ❏ 1. I know how to get my children into Little League, piano lessons, soccer, etc.
- ❏ 2. I know how to properly set a table.
- ❏ 3. I know which stores are most likely to carry the clothing brands my family wears.
- ❏ 4. My children know the best name brands in clothing.
- ❏ 5. I know how to order in a nice restaurant.
- ❏ 6. I know how to use a credit card, checking account, and saving account—and I understand an annuity. I understand term life insurance, disability insurance, and 20/80 medical insurance, as well as house insurance, flood insurance, and replacement insurance.
- ❏ 7. I talk to my children about going to college.
- ❏ 8. I know how to get one of the best interest rates on my new car loan.
- ❏ 9. I understand the difference among the principal, interest, and escrow statements on my house payment.
- ❏ 10. I know how to help my children with their homework and do not hesitate to call the school if I need additional information.
- ❏ 11. I know how to decorate the house for the different holidays.
- ❏ 12. I know how to get a library card.
- ❏ 13. I know how to use the different tools in the garage.
- ❏ 14. I repair items in my house almost immediately when they break—or know a repair service and call it.

COULD YOU SURVIVE IN WEALTH?

Put a check by each item you know how to do.

- ❏ 1. I can read a menu in French, English, and another language.

❏ 2. I have several favorite restaurants in different countries of the world.

❏ 3. During the holidays, I know how to hire a decorator to identify the appropriate themes and items with which to decorate the house.

❏ 4. I know who my preferred financial advisor, legal service, designer, domestic employment service, and hairdresser are.

❏ 5. I have at least two residences that are staffed and maintained.

❏ 6. I know how to ensure confidentiality and loyalty from my domestic staff.

❏ 7. I have at least two or three "screens" that keep people whom I do not wish to see away from me.

❏ 8. I fly in my own plane, the company plane, or the *Concorde*.

❏ 9. I know how to enroll my children in the preferred private schools.

❏ 10. I know how to host the parties that "key" people attend.

❏ 11. I am on the boards of at least two charities.

❏ 12. I know the hidden rules of the Junior League.

❏ 13. I support or buy the work of a particular artist.

❏ 14. I know how to read a corporate financial statement and analyze my own financial statements.

(Reprinted by permission. Take from *A Framework for Understanding Poverty* by Ruby K. Payne, 1-800-424-9484)

- In which economic class do you feel most comfortable?
- Reflect on the reasons you are more at home in that class culture.
- How well would you succeed in the other class cultures?

The first point about this exercise is that if you fall mostly in the middle class, the assumption is that everyone knows these things. However, if you did not know many of the items for the other classes, the exercise points out how many of the hidden rules are taken for granted by a particular class, which assumes they are understood by everyone.

Personal action plan

1. Name some of your congregational mental models—unspoken and often unconscious ways of doing things.
   - Reflect on these in relation to people in generational poverty. Remember that all generalizations have exceptions and not all people in generational poverty are the same or show uniform characteristics.
   - However, with that caveat, identify one or two of your congregation's mental models that could be a barrier for someone coming out of a different cultural class than your own. Some examples of unspoken mental models that might act as barriers would be "Everyone knows and understands the liturgy." Or "We are all best friends in the congregation."
   - What might you do to change that mental model into a more welcoming practice?
2. Identify some of the hidden rules at your work place or in a community setting. Make a list of those rules and discuss them with a trusted colleague.
3. Read all or parts of several of the books referred to in this chapter.
4. Determine one plan of action that you feel called to do as a result of your exploration of the topics in this chapter. Ask someone to hold you accountable for following through with your plan.
5. Talk with business people and teachers and ask if they have noticed differences between people coming out of various economic classes.

Getting together with others

1. Discuss "A Little Quiz" and where you found yourself in this exercise.

- What are the implications for you and for your congregation?
2. Read together the passage on "Mental Models" from Peter Senge's book, *The Fifth Discipline: The Art and Practice of the Learning Organization.* Then look at the description of Harold's congregation, Christ the King. Identify some of the possible mental models in his congregation.
   - Would you think that his congregation exhibits the hidden rules (mental models) of one particular economic class?
   - If so, which one? Discuss your reasons.
3. Identify and discuss some of your congregation's mental models.
   - Do these mental models reveal any barriers to mission among people in generational poverty?
   - What would need to change in order for your congregation to be a welcoming place for people from poverty?
4. Discuss Ephesians 2:11-22.
   - What does this text say about the mission that God is calling your congregation to do?
5. Together watch the movie *Sister Act* starring Whoopi Goldberg. After you have viewed it, identify the mental models that shaped the culture of the congregation "B.D." (before Delores) and "A.D." (after Delores). Discuss the implications for your own congregation.
6. Together begin to formulate a plan of action for your congregation and/or community based on the first three chapters.
   - Map out the steps in your plan.
   - Who will lead in each step?
   - Agree to hold one another mutually accountable for the plan.
7. Examine "A Common Foundation: Shared Principles for Work on Overcoming Poverty" (see page 13) and consider these statements as mental models.
   - How could they shape the public life of a community or a state?

4

A Systems View:
We are One Community

Marge's story

As Marge turned off the county road for the last part of the drive home, she glanced at the clock on the dashboard. "Huh," she chuckled, "5:21 on the dot; same as always." She left work at approximately 5:05 each day and always seemed to be making this turn at precisely 5:21—except on those days that she did grocery shopping after work or on days when she was driving through a heavy snowstorm. She drove up the lane to the farmhouse where she knew Gene would be about halfway through the evening's milking process.

Marge and Gene lived on Marge's family farm where they had lived all of their married life. Marge—and Gene—had been the sole inheritor of the farm because her older brother had died in a car accident when he was a sophomore in college and her younger sister had married and moved out of state. They had lived with her parents in the large old farmhouse and had been working the farm for thirty-three years—first with her parents, then, as Mom and Dad got older and finally passed away, by themselves. Both Marge and Gene loved the farm—even though they had inherited the farm debt along with the land. In recent years they had begun to wonder if the farm was more blessing or curse.

Both Marge and Gene knew the only way they could be farming and run the dairy was because they had inherited it. They knew they never could have had the resources to have bought the land, the house, and the whole operation. And even with the land and the house being passed on to them, still Marge had been working at the bank for twenty-three years now to try to make ends meet, to try to decrease their ever-present debt load, and to pay for college for Dan (now thirty-one, married with two beautiful little girls, and working in the city) and Denise (twenty-eight, single, and working in Colorado Springs).

Each year Marge and Gene wondered how long they could hold on to the farm. Instead of their debt load decreasing, they were actually more in debt now than ten years ago. How was that possible? The truth was that they just weren't making it. At best they were holding on, but only by that proverbial "thread." Every year when they paid their property taxes, they were reminded how much the land value had increased, how expenses had increased, while prices for milk and other farm produce had been stagnant for years. She knew that the bank was as lenient as possible with their loan payments because she was a valued worker at the bank.

Marge was often thankful that her parents were not alive to see the dilemma and the hard choices they were facing. She and Gene had hoped they would have ten more good years to get out of debt and to figure out what to do with the farm after they were gone, but in reality they both knew they couldn't avoid making some difficult decisions soon. They were fairly certain that neither Dan nor Denise would want to come back and carry on the farming tradition, which wasn't really an option now anyway. They also knew they could easily sell the farm to a developer who would divide the land into "country estates" and sell them to families from the city who didn't mind driving an hour each way to work. Knowing that, they kept pushing away any decision. They fully realized how deeply they were in debt; the farm was just not paying for itself, much less making a living for them. Without Marge's job they knew they would have had to face selling the farm a long time ago. But the idea of selling the farm to a developer just didn't feel right. This was a farm and should be kept as a working farm, not broken up into lots for city folks who wanted the peace and quiet of the countryside and the amenities of city life. Besides, they faced an ethical dilemma here too. If they sold their farm to a developer, their neighbors' way of life—and their tax rates—could be affected, and that just didn't seem like the right thing to do to people they had known their whole lives.

As Marge pulled the car into the garage she thought maybe that she would bring up this whole dilemma after supper. They couldn't put it off much longer. But first she would see how Gene's day had gone.

Marge's journal
Monday

Well, we didn't talk. When I got home I could see right away that Gene had had a very bad day and wouldn't be in any mood to talk about tough decisions. The tractor had broken down when he was in the middle of planting, and one of our best producing cows is sick and he had to call the vet. That means she's out of production for at least a week. Gene didn't get into the house until almost 9:00 and we ate supper and watched the news and weather. Gene did tell me all that had happened, and that's at least a good sign when he's willing to discuss things. Perhaps tomorrow we'll get into the future plans.

Tuesday

I just can't believe it! I still can't believe it! Here we haven't wanted to sell our land to the developers because of what that would mean for our neighbors, and today at the bank I found out that the Schmidts, our neighbors to the south, have done just that—and not even told us first. I feel so betrayed! When I told Gene this evening, he was just as frustrated and angry as I am. I don't know what we will do when we have to see the Schmidts tomorrow evening at church. I don't know how I can be friends with them after this.

Well, at least that meant we couldn't put off our discussion any longer. This news prompted us to start talking seriously about what we need to do. We even looked at our financial statements together for a change. Truth is that we're losing the farm. There, I said it (or wrote it). We are so far in debt that we can barely keep up with the loan payments, and sometimes we're behind on those. The options we have aren't the greatest, but we realize we have to look at them now. We know that the option of doing nothing will only lead to foreclosure, and the other options are to sell or rent the farm to someone who will continue to farm it, or to sell to a developer. If we can't make a go of farming we don't think anyone else can either. Besides, if we rent, the rent wouldn't even pay the taxes and loan payments. That doesn't leave many options before us.

Wednesday

This was a tough evening with a lot of confusing feelings. The Schmidts were indeed at the church event, and we couldn't avoid them. In fact, Joan came up to me as soon as she saw me. She told me what their dilemma has been and it sounds a lot like our situation. She apologized for not saying anything before the sale went through, but she hinted that John was simply ashamed of having to sell the farm and didn't want anyone to know. I guess I can understand that and can't hold that against them. Anyway, I am so glad that we talked because Joan and John have always been good friends and good neighbors as well as church members.

But, the other thing that happened this evening was more difficult. I met one of the new families from the city, the Millers, who just bought one of the "country estates" and are building their home out here in the "peaceful countryside where their children can breathe the fresh air and experience the wonders of rural life." I almost choked and had a very hard time being cordial. Here we are in a situation where we may lose our farm, partly because of the very people like the Millers, and now they're even invading our church! Oh, dear, I know that sounds so mean-spirited and unwelcoming, but I have to say the negative thoughts somewhere. God, I hope you will forgive my mixed-up feelings.

Thursday

Tonight we called Dan and, later, Denise and told them about the difficult financial situation we are in. We asked both of them the same thing we've asked before—whether either of them think they would want to come back and live on the farm at any time in the future. Both said they love the farm but their careers will probably mean they would not live here. That is what we had thought, but we needed to make sure. We then mentioned that we are seriously considering selling the farm to the same developer who bought the Schmidts' farm. Denise didn't seem too bothered by that possibility, but Dan and his family love to come out for visits. Dan likes to show the cows to the girls and tell them how he used to help with the milking and other chores. Dan is someone who likes the idea of farming but doesn't want the reality of farming. I guess I can't blame him. Besides, it's better that they don't have their heart set on coming back to farm.

Both Dan and Denise were supportive of any decision we need to make. That at least gives Gene and me some encouragement. After we talked to both of them, we called the developer and made an appointment for him to come over on Saturday afternoon. Wow, a lot has happened in less than a week. My feelings are still all mixed up. I'm sure we will be sorting them out for a while. If we decide to sell, then we need to decide what Gene will do and whether we will buy or build a house in town.

Friday

Well, I guess I'm not finished discovering new things for the week. I went by the church today to pick up my committee minutes, and I ran into a young woman just walking out of the church. I had seen her a couple of times at the checkout counter at the discount store, but I really never thought she might live around here. Well, we started talking a bit, and I could tell she was pretty down. Her name is Rita and she lives in the trailer park at the edge of town. I was a bit embarrassed to realize that she is the first person that I have ever met from the trailer park, even though I drive by it every day. I don't think I ever thought of the people who live there as being part of our community—and especially not part of our congregation's community.

As we talked a bit, she told me some of her situation. She and her husband and two children moved to the trailer park three years ago. They thought they could make a better living out here because they couldn't find jobs in the city. At the beginning they both found work—she as a checkout clerk and he as a carpenter. But then a year ago, her husband suddenly left, and she's been trying to make it on only her income. She's worried because her son has been ill and her health insurance will no longer cover his medication. She told me she was grateful that the church had given her some help with this month's prescription. After she mentioned that, I did have the good sense to invite her and the children back to worship on Sunday. She sounded like they might come.

For me that was a significant conversation. Gene and I have been so worried about what we will do about the farm that I have not been able to see the situation of others. God, you may be opening my eyes in a variety of ways. I guess I want you to continue to do that. Thank you for this crazy, mixed-up life we have. Let me trust you to lead and guide us. And take care of Rita and her children. I wonder how many other Ritas there are right here in our community.

Saturday

I found Rita at the checkout counter this morning when I was shopping. She remembered our conversation, and I again invited her and the children to Sunday school and worship tomorrow. I think they might actually come. I told her I would meet them at the door fifteen minutes before worship begins and show them around. She seemed pleased—as well as a bit nervous.

Then this afternoon the developer came for our appointment. Gene and I listened to his offer, and he asked quite a few questions. He's really not such a bad guy, but it's just what he represents that I don't like. After he left, neither Gene nor I was ready to talk, so we agreed that we would think about it tonight, pray for God to lead us, and tomorrow afternoon we'll have a conversation about what we think we should do. It's sort of strange in a way, but ever since I met Rita yesterday and heard her story, I've begun to think that we are facing some similar kinds of challenges—just from different perspectives. That doesn't make it any better, but for some reason I feel more at peace and more determined to do something that helps people like the Schmidts and Rita as well as Gene and me.

Going deeper
We are one community

Central city, suburban, and rural issues are cut from the same fabric. What affects one area affects the other areas. Either they all prosper together or they languish together. Many of the difficult decisions that Marge and Gene are facing in the episode have been caused by dynamics in the central cities and suburbs of their metropolitan area. As people with means have moved out of the central city (for a variety of reasons), they have taken their resources with them. Availability of jobs has followed this outward movement, and the result is a depressed central city. As people with means move further and further away from the city core, services follow, and developers see an opportunity for financial gain and continue to push the edges ever outward into rural and farming areas.

Farmland, the tax rate for which was previously based solely on agricultural production, is eventually revalued. While the tax rate on farmland continues to be protected in many states, tax rates can still rise for all property owners because of the increased demand for local services. As housing developments spring up in once agricultural areas, sewer systems, roads, schools, and other necessities of suburban life also spread. The effect on farmers can be an increase in tax rates, while the effect on the central city is a decrease in available subsidy for sewer and transportation systems and other resources. In essence the central city loses the resources that subsidize the new housing developments.

When this outward sprawl takes place, both residents of the central city and farmers in the rural areas lose. Resources leave the central cities, which depresses the inner core for the entire metropolitan region. At the same time, the value of land and demand for services increase to such a degree that the only viable option farmers may have is to sell to developers. So the cycle continues unabated.

Two maps on the Web site www.ameregis.com (see the maps for twenty-five different urban areas) show the "Tax Capacity per Household, 1998" and "Percentage Change in Tax Capacity per Household, 1993–1998." These two maps give a picture of how the land values have increased in the outer areas of metropolitan regions. A third map, "Change in Urbanized Area, 1970–1990," gives a clear picture of the outward spread of housing developments into the rural areas. If a map would show the further change into the present, the trend of urban sprawl would be undoubtedly even more striking.

Key passages in the Bible (see "Bible Study" below) give a clear message that God created and intended for people to live in community and care for one another. Isaiah 24 depicts the "city of chaos" while Isaiah 25, picturing the "mountain of the Lord," makes clear that God's promises are meant for *all*. First Corinthians 12 speaks in terms of "one body." Ephesians 2:11-22 tells how dividing walls of hostility have been broken down by the cross of Jesus Christ, reconciling all into one body. We are "no longer strangers and aliens, but . . . citizens with the saints and also members of the household of God . . . with Christ Jesus himself as the cornerstone. In him the whole structure is joined together" (vv. 19-21).

One additional aspect to consider in rural and small town communities is that of the invisible poor. These are the people who work on the farms or in the service industry in jobs that do not pay livable wages. These are the people who live in the trailer park or the rundown housing area in town or country—the area that has always been there but that is not consciously thought of as part of the community. These are the pockets of poverty that need to be noticed, acknowledged, and included in God's *all*, for God's word articulates a clear concern that we are of one community and what affects one affects us all.

The "bottom line," then, is that what is good, healthy, just for the central city and suburbs is also good, healthy, just for rural areas and vice versa. What is needed is a wise regional approach to sustainable growth and revitalization for central city, suburbs, and rural-small town areas, for, indeed, *we are one community!*

Bible study

Read Isaiah 24:1-13 and Isaiah 25:1-10.

Describe the "city of chaos" in Isaiah 24 and the "mountain of the Lord" in Isaiah 25.

Both scenarios apply to "all."

What are the implications for ending poverty in your community or state?

Read 1 Corinthians 12:12-27

How does this text relate to "A Common Foundation: Shared Principles for Work on Overcoming Poverty"? (See page 13.)

Give examples of how what happens in one part of the body (or community) directly or indirectly affects what happens in the other parts.

Read Ephesians 2:11-22.

Tell your own stories about how the cross of Jesus Christ has broken down dividing walls of hostility.

How does this passage relate to the point in this chapter that we are all one community?

How could this passage be lived out in the metropolitan region?

How does it relate to tensions in a congregation between "new" people and those who have been around much longer?

Resources

American Research and Geographic Information Systems Web site: www.ameregis.com

Duncan, Cynthia M. *Worlds Apart: Why Poverty Persists in Rural America.* New Haven, Conn.: Yale University Press, 2000.

Lyson, Thomas A. and William W. Falk, eds. *Forgotten Places: Uneven Development and the Loss of Opportunity in Rural America.* Lawrence, Kan.: University Press of Kansas, 1993.

Minnesotans for an Energy-Efficient Economy Web site: www.me3.org/projects/sprawl

"We Are One Community," Bible study on Isaiah 24–25, first presented at the 2003 Saint Paul Area Synod Assembly: www.spaselca.org/aboutsynod/poverty/nm-bspoverty.htm

Perspectives

From Martin Luther King Jr.'s *Strength to Love* (Philadelphia: Fortress Press, 1963), p. 70:

> In a real sense, all life is interrelated. All [people] are caught in an inescapable network of mutuality, tied in a single garment of destiny. Whatever affects one directly affects all indirectly. I can never be what I ought to be until you are what you ought to be, and you can never be what you ought to be until I am what I ought to be. This is the interrelated structure of reality.

Banks were foreclosing on tenant farmers, and everyone became victim to the system. The following is a conversation between the owner man and the tenant farmer (from John Steinbeck's *The Grapes of Wrath* [New York: Viking Press, 1939], p. 45):

> "We're sorry. It's not us. It's the monster. The bank isn't like a man."
>
> "Yes, but the bank is only made of men."
>
> "No, you're wrong there—quite wrong there. The bank is something else than men. It happens that every man in a bank hates what the bank does, and yet the bank does it. The bank is something more than men, I tell you. It's the monster. Men made it, but they can't control it."

From "What Would Jesus Do? Sock It to Alabama's Corporate Landowners," Abstract, by Adam Cohen. *Editorial Observer* (June 10, 2003), p. 28:

> Editorial Observer reports that Alabama's teetotaling, Bible-quoting Gov Bob Riley has stunned conservative supporters by pushing through tax reform, using stark moral argument that Christians are prohibited from oppressing the poor; says ratification by voters would be major victory for poor people in state where tax system is brutally weighted against them; also sees pointed challenge to groups that strive to inject their Christian values into national policy. If the religious right had called up Central Casting last year to fill the part of governor, it could hardly have done better than the teetotaling, Bible-quoting businessman from rural central Alabama who now heads up the state. As a Republican congressman, Bob Riley had a nearly perfect record of opposing any legislation supported by the liberal Americans for Democratic Action.
>
> But Governor Riley has stunned many of his conservative supporters, and enraged the state's powerful farm and timber

lobbies, by pushing a tax reform plan through the Alabama Legislature that shifts a significant amount of the state's tax burden from the poor to wealthy individuals and corporations. And he has framed the issue in starkly moral terms, arguing that the current Alabama tax system violates biblical teachings because Christians are prohibited from oppressing the poor.

Regarding the phenomenon of urban sprawl, Orfield writes (from Myron Orfield's *American Metropolitics: The New Suburban Reality*, pp. 63, 129-130):

In the future, better data are likely to be available to compare regional urban development trends to factors such as social separation and fiscal inequality. . . . This section hints that regions using land far in excess of population growth increase the level of stress not only on the communities left behind, but also on the communities developing at the edge. The future may show that unduly sprawling regions are "growing against themselves" and in the process are hurting all types of regional communities and all citizens. . . .

Persistent urban poverty, increasing traffic congestion, and the relentless pressure to develop open space and farmland have made the public uneasy about urban growth. Many are demanding action from their representatives in local, state, and national government. Because of the fragmented nature of governance in America's metropolitan regions, however, local representatives are ill-equipped to meet regional challenges. . . . Growing awareness of these inefficiencies and the inequities fostered by governmental structures has led to a resurgence of support for some form of regional governance. Evidence of the continued interdependence between cities and their surrounding suburbs and of the heightened importance of regional efficiency and productivity in the competitive global economy provides additional economic incentives for cities to abandon parochial laws and attitudes in favor of collaboration and, ultimately, structural reform of government systems.

Learning more about Marge's congregation
St. John's Lutheran, a rural-urban fringe congregation
Description by Craig Van Gelder

This congregation is a historical rural-village church that was originally located thirty-five miles from the major city. St. John's was started in the 1890s by German farm families and located in a village that by the 1920s had become a town of thirteen hundred people. Services continued to be held in the native language until World War II, when they changed to English. However, the church has a long-standing tradition of celebrating its German heritage for a weekend each July when it returns to a native-language service along with other festivities. Many visitors from throughout the metropolitan area attend that event.

St. John's membership grew to about five hundred members during the 1920s and remained at that level for decades. However, in the past two decades the church has experienced some modest growth due to the large number of new families who are moving into the various subdivisions being built nearby. Most of the newcomers to the church are Lutheran transfers, but they tend to be more educated and middle-class than the people they are joining. These new members soon find out they are joining a congregation that consists largely of three extended families that have intermarried over the years. In the past few years, some tension has begun to surface in the congregation over worship style, but it is clear that the sides are primarily formed along the lines of new comers versus historic members.

Moving into action
Reflecting on your own experience

1. Think of people you have known who have been forced to face difficult decisions similar to the ones faced by Marge and Gene.
   - What were the underlying systemic issues or dynamics that may have contributed to the situation?
2. Marge realized that she had driven by the trailer park every day but did not think of the people in the trailer park as part of the community or her congregation's community.
   - Are there people in your own community who are hidden, or invisible, to you and to your congregation?
   - If so, who are they?
3. What are some of the most difficult decisions you have had to make? Who supported you? Who provided resources during these periods of time?
4. How is Marge and Gene's situation related to Rita's situation? Reflect on the connection between rural poverty and central city concentrations of poverty.

Personal action plan

1. Research further information on the effects of central-city sprawl into the rural-small town areas. Visit the Web site www.ameregis. com to study the regional maps for several urban areas.
   - What are some of your conclusions?
   - What are some of your questions?
2. Gene and Marge were facing difficult decisions; however they did have options. Because they lived close to a metropolitan area, they could sell their land and make a profit. Other farmers in rural areas based solely on an agricultural economy may not have any positive options when farm prices (still at fifty-year-old levels, especially for corn) continue to lag while expenses continue to increase.

- Listen to the stories of farmers who are near a metropolitan area as well as those more distant from an urban center.
- What are the differences and similarities in their situations?

Getting together with others

1. Discuss your congregation's setting in relation to that of Gene and Marge's congregation, St. John's.
   - What are some of the dynamics between the long-time members and the newcomers?
   - Has your congregation experienced any similar challenges or tensions?
2. Discuss the several manifestations of poverty presented in this chapter—rural farmers, the invisible poor within a community, and the related systemic causes of poverty.
   - What are the implications for mission and action in the statement, "We are one community"?
3. Read and discuss the points of view represented in the section, "Perspectives" on page 91-93.
   - How are all of these related to the theme, "We are one community"?
   - What troubles you or causes tension in any of these quotes?
   - What gives you hope?
4. Review the different aspects of poverty presented in these four chapters.
   - How are they all related?
   - What are the various causes of poverty that you have discovered?
5. Have you identified any new insights for you and for your congregation's mission? If so, discuss those insights. How will you act on those insights?

Appendix

Ending Poverty: A Biblical Moral Mandate within Civil Society

*A Process for Mobilizing and Engaging
Congregations based on "A Common Foundation:
Shared Principles for Work on Overcoming Poverty"*

Background

In 2001, the Saint Paul Area Synod of the Evangelical Lutheran Church in America adopted a threefold vision:

- To equip ten thousand leaders to be catalysts for mission
- To invite all to hear the story of Jesus
- To end poverty so that no one is forced to live in poverty

Three leadership teams were formed to guide the work of the synod to accomplish the vision. Each leadership team was made up of eight to twelve people, with one representative of the synod council and a synod staff person relating to each team. The responsibility for organizing and developing the work of each part of the vision was given to the leadership teams. All three teams began their work with vigor and trepidation, understanding full well the weight of the task that had been handed to them.

My involvement

My call to join the staff of Bishop Peter Rogness and the Saint Paul Area Synod began in November 2002, a year after the teams had begun their work. Within the bishop's staff, as we together determined various responsibilities of the synod staff, it was decided that I would relate to two of the leadership teams: the "Inviting" team and the "Ending Poverty" team. I was pleased.

All of the teams had begun their work in earnest. Talented and committed people were serving on each team, and plans were beginning to be developed.

Ending poverty leadership team

The Ending Poverty Leadership Team had developed some of the most creative plans while experiencing by far the most tension:

- Do we end poverty by increasing acts of charity and service among our congregations, or do we focus on advocacy and justice in the public arena?
- Do we work with individuals in congregations, or work with each congregation of the synod, or do we put our energies into faith-based community-organizing efforts?
- Is ending poverty a part of one's personal faith commitment, or is it a goal that gets one involved in the political arena? Furthermore, are one's personal faith commitment, on the one hand, and involvement in the political arena, on the other, compatible? Or are they mutually exclusive?
- Oh, and one more question to grapple with: Do we dare even think that ending poverty is possible within the Saint Paul area or anywhere?

A major breakthrough had occurred before my tenure began. The team had decided to address poverty in three arenas—education, service, and advocacy—with the initial focus on lack of affordable housing in the Twin Cities area.

A second breakthrough came in the summer of 2003, eight months after my work in the synod began. This breakthrough must have been the work of the Holy Spirit at the end of a frustrating all-day retreat of the Ending Poverty team. The retreat had been planned with the sole purpose of coming together around a plan that had been drafted by several members of the team, with input from others. I had put the plan on paper and thought it represented the various points of view represented by team members.

When presented during the retreat, the plan fell flat. With the retreat dragging toward an end, tension and fatigue permeated the room.

Out of desperation and with only one hour of the retreat left, the suggestion was made that we place the plan on hold and, instead, attempt to write down our mental models (ala Peter Senge in *The Fifth Discipline*) to which we could all agree. After an amazingly brief time, and with team members more engaged than at any time that day, we developed the mental models that could guide future work:

Because:

- Christian Scriptures reveal a God who has provided for everyone.
- Christian Scriptures reveal God's expectations for those who have the world's goods and those who do not.

Therefore:

- Ending poverty is possible.
- Everything we need to end poverty is at hand.
- Congregations are a powerful force for positive change within their community contexts and in the world.

And we are called to make audacious commitments:

- Every person has the right to accessible resources.
- All people, and especially children, have a right to decent housing, health care, and education.
- Jobs should pay adequate wages to provide food, shelter, and other necessities.
- Everyone needs accessible transportation for work.
- A sufficient supply of supportive and transitional housing, adequately staffed, should be available.

And to live our faith as church in the world:

- The Saint Paul Area Synod, congregations, individuals, and communities will act publicly to make systemic change.

- This vision to end poverty and these commitments will be known throughout the Saint Paul area.

    With these mental models we were finally ready to go forward together.

Advocacy subgroup

The next significant step forward came as a suggestion from the synod council representative on the team. Even with valuable agreement on the mental models, we now had to grapple with the most appropriate and effective methods by which to live out these mental models. During one of these prolonged discussions, the synod council representative suggested that we have three subgroups focused on the three emphases of education, service, and advocacy—each contributing toward the goal of ending poverty. Each subgroup could invite additional members, carry out its particular work, and report back to the full leadership team. People on the team could choose the subgroup to which they felt most committed.

Everyone on the leadership team rallied around this suggestion, resulting in the birth of two (instead of three) subgroups: the Education/Service subgroup and the Advocacy subgroup, each with its own chair who was also a member of the leadership team.

"A Common Foundation: Shared Principles for Work on Overcoming Poverty"

In November 2003 three of us sat around the table in my office. We had been charged with the task of drafting a plan for engaging congregations in advocacy to end poverty. We were to present the draft at the next Advocacy subgroup meeting.

One part of the plan dealt with the proposal that, instead of involving individuals in congregations or even congregations on a one-by-one basis, we would attempt to engage and mobilize *clusters* of congregations to work together to end poverty in their particular area and in the Saint Paul area as a whole.

However, we were still very much aware of the divergent opinions among our Ending Poverty Leadership Team as to what actions were most appropriate for a faith-based effort and what plans would have the best possibility of making a difference in ending poverty.

A few days prior to our meeting, I had been on a flight home from a conference. Troubled by the continuing friction slowing our progress, I began to wonder if a set of statements (or mental models) could be drafted that people of all different political as well as faith traditions could agree on and that could form the foundation for work on ending poverty across political, economic, and religious differences. At our meeting, the three of us discussed this idea of a set of statements and decided to pose the question to Bishop Rogness as to whether he might convene a group of religious leaders to draft such a "manifesto." I left the meeting to test out the question with the bishop, and before I finished describing our idea, he was already jotting down thoughts for the statements. Before I left his office, he requested a copy of the mental models we had developed at the leadership retreat. He wanted to use these statements as a starting point for writing the shared principles.

The birth date for "A Common Foundation: Shared Principles for Work on Overcoming Poverty" was fall 2003. On March 31, 2004, a press conference was held and thirty-four religious leaders in the state of Minnesota signed on to this document—leaders from a broad ecumenical spectrum as well as leaders from Jewish, Muslim, and Hindu faith traditions.

Two paths for working together in clusters

The development of "Common Foundation" (as it has come to be known) was the real breakthrough we needed. Everyone on the Ending Poverty Leadership Team could agree with these statements. Both the Education/Service subgroup and the Advocacy subgroup could use this document to guide their work. But, as we soon realized, living out the statements and "giving them legs" would become the most challenging and rewarding part of our work toward ending poverty.

We decided that our strategy for working in congregational clusters was a valid one. We then developed "two paths for working together in clusters": an Education and Service Path entitled "Engaging and Mobilizing Clusters of Congregations in Education and Service" and a Justice and Advocacy Path called "Ending Poverty through Faithful Citizenship."

The Advocacy subgroup agreed that the "Common Foundation" would serve as (1) a lens through which to assess the legislative agenda for 2005 and (2) a plan for action.

My primary work became meeting with individual pastors (1) to listen to their own hopes and plans for mission in their congregation and (2) to present our plan for Ending Poverty through Faithful Citizenship. If there was a convergence in mission planning, I invited the pastor to bring two to three members of their congregation to a meeting where we would present further information on a path toward systemic change. All of the pastors I visited were pastors of congregations that were not already involved in ISAIAH, the faith-based community-organizing effort in the Twin Cities.

Over a period of several months, I had one-on-one conversations with approximately forty pastors. Most of them either attended, or identified several lay leaders in their congregations to attend, the first gathering of potential cluster congregations on May 25, 2004. At this meeting we outlined a path toward working together with congregations that were already a part of ISAIAH, especially by participating in a large "Faith in Democracy" preelection event in October, as well as looking ahead to the state legislative agenda and how "A Common Foundation" might be lived into reality.

Clusters

The makeup and naming of clusters evolved over a period of several months. The names simply were a description of their geographic area. For example, "Central Cluster" was used to describe the cluster in the central area of Saint Paul; the "97/95/8 Cluster" used the names of three highways along which that group of congregations were located. We began working with eight clusters, which continued to expand into other areas as well. Most of the clusters were made up of ELCA congregations, but at least three of the clusters developed as ecumenical clusters from their inception.

The definition of a cluster, initially, was fluid, and it has continued to be so. A congregation that is considered to be a part of a cluster simply means that a passionate few (or many) in a congregation have a commitment to bring their faith into the public arena in order to work toward ending poverty in their area and in the state. Sometimes the pastor—or one of the pastors—is directly involved. In other congregations the involvement is completely instigated and led by the group of members. In all cases the pastor(s) are informed and supportive of the work.

Ending poverty "Road show"

Also during the spring of 2004 we developed what became affectionately known as our "road show." The proper name for the three-hour workshop was "Called to End Poverty" with the outline:

- The Vision: present "A 20/20 Vision for Ending Poverty"
- The Context: educate about the culture of poverty, using Ruby Payne's material on *A Framework for Understanding Poverty*
- God's Call: present "A Common Foundation: Shared Principles for Overcoming Poverty" and the reasons that we need to bring our faith into the public arena
- Our Response: give opportunity for response through charity and service or advocacy and justice

We presented this workshop at a preassembly gathering of one hundred and again in July for approximately eighty people from eight developing clusters of congregations. Momentum was building and congregations were getting involved.

Faith in democracy

Our goal was to have 200 from the cluster congregations attend the ISAIAH-sponsored "Faith in Democracy" event on October 10, 2004. One month prior to the big event, on September 16, we held a "Pre-Faith in Democracy" gathering for the cluster participants. Bishop Peter Rogness recounted Lutheran tradition, which not only allows but, in a sense, propels the church into the public arena. We made our plans to take our faith into Roy Wilkens Arena in downtown Saint Paul on October 10.

For the "Faith in Democracy" event, we counted 160, not 200, but a good contribution, nevertheless, for our newly born clusters. The total attendance from all parts of the faith community in the Twin Cities area was more than four thousand, and the legislators, as well as everyone who attended, were inspired and amazed at such a turnout showing people of faith bringing their hopes and convictions for justice into the democratic process. As part of the program for the event, Bishop Rogness presented "A Common Foundation," which was also a part of the printed agenda.

Public policy assessment tool

At the July "Called to End Poverty" workshop for the clusters, one idea that the Advocacy subgroup was working on was reported—the idea that "A Common Foundation" could serve as the lens through which to assess past legislative decisions as well as engage in dialogue with legislators about their positions on various issues that affect people in poverty. Several congregation members in attendance virtually jumped at the further opportunity to develop a Public Policy Assessment Tool, based on "A Common Foundation," to be used in candidate forums and conversations with candidates. An ad hoc committee of eight passionate and knowledgeable people created this document entitled "Building on a Common Foundation: Public Policy Assessment Tool." The six areas of the first shared principle (adequate food and shelter, meaningful work, safe communities, health care, and education) became the focus for the assessment tool. Under each of those broad topics, specific background facts and candidate questions were developed.

In addition to the background material and questions, the second section of the assessment tool was the "Biblical Foundation for Ending Poverty." In this section we "offered a selection of passages that Christians can use to equip themselves for the challenging but essential work of bringing their faith into their politics in pursuit of both love and justice for the neighbor." What followed were selected passages that addressed the themes from "A Common Foundation" and which left no doubt about God's call to faithfully care for and about those living in poverty.

Eight-month strategy

Post "Faith in Democracy" event (October 10, 2004) and pre-election day (November 2, 2004), we knew we needed to turn our attention to the state legislative agenda, regardless of the outcome of national and state elections. One member of the Advocacy subgroup drafted an "Eight-month strategy for clusters," the eight months being from November 3, 2004, through June 2005 (the scheduled ending for the state legislative session). The Advocacy subgroup decided to bring together a representative group from all of the clusters to hear and discuss the proposed plan. We scheduled the date for that meeting to be November 3, a date that we hoped would convey that we were committed to working with whomever would turn out to be our elected public leaders. More than thirty people gathered to discuss the draft of the eight-month strategy, and what a discussion it was! The momentum and the commitment were almost palpable in the room. People were engaged.

(On a side note, I had experienced a retina detachment in my left eye earlier that morning, but, when I called to schedule a doctor's appointment, I chose the very last possible appointment time that day so that I could stay for most of the discussion. It was worth the postponement.)

We named the eight-month strategy "Ending Poverty: A Biblical Moral Mandate within Civil Society"—to make the statement that we see the biblical call to end poverty as the most clearly-given mandate from God to people of faith. Also, after an election process that focused much attention on a discussion about personal morality, we wanted to give witness to our view that ending poverty is of utmost importance for a public morality.

The eight-month strategy for clusters centered around three all-cluster gatherings, each with a joint legislative strategy. Each gathering would have the same four ingredients:

- Renew and refresh our commitment to "A Common Foundation: Shared Principles for Work on Overcoming Poverty"
- Education on the legislative process and our focus issues (see below)
- Immediate Action—which turned out to be writing letters to our legislators and the governor
- Next Steps—within each cluster and as a whole

With much work and passion and joy, with a spirit of collaboration and collegiality, the three all-cluster gatherings became realities.

"Claiming a Moral Public Agenda"—December 6, 2004

The purpose was to prepare for the upcoming state legislative session. We heard the budget forecast for the state and invited three state legislators (two Democrats and one Republican) to speak about how we could be most effective in working with legislators and influencing decisions.

"Introducing a Moral Public Agenda"—February 14, 2005

At this gathering we learned more about the governor's proposed budget and discussed the two focus issues that were on the legislative agenda and that we knew greatly affected people living in poverty: (1) early childhood development and (2) health care. We identified legislators working on key committees associated with our two focus issues and the legislative districts that they represented.

"Achieving a Moral Public Agenda"—March 31, 2005

The purpose of this gathering was to make clear plans within each cluster regarding how to stay in contact with our legislators on a weekly basis for the remainder of the legislative session. Our letter writing regarding the two focus issues now contained specific bill numbers that we supported.

Twelve disciples

At the December 6 all-cluster gathering, one of the legislators had made an almost offhand comment: "You know if you had ten people in each legislative district in the whole state asking for the same thing, you could get anything you wanted."

And the lights went on for several of us! Why couldn't we do just that? We had been searching for an effective way to organize our work, and this just might be the organizing strategy. From that comment we developed our "12 disciples plan." We asked each cluster to be responsible for the legislative districts in which their cluster churches were located. Then we asked each cluster to identify twelve "disciples" in each of those legislative districts. These twelve disciples would work together to plan their weekly contact with their legislator and advocate our two issues—early childhood development and health care—both integral to "A Common Foundation."

By the March 31, 2005, gathering most of the legislative districts in the Saint Paul area were covered with at least several disciples staying in contact with their legislators. Some districts had many disciples with legislators who long ago had committed their support to our focus issues. Other districts had only a few working with legislators who were not as supportive. Nevertheless, we knew we had "stumbled" onto a strategy that had real possibilities for the future.

Measurements of faith-filled success

In preparation for the March gathering we developed a document by which to measure our success. We included the following five criteria:

1. Twelve disciples will have been identified and engaged in the legislative process from each of the legislative districts within the Saint Paul area—and the state.
2. A strategy for staying in contact with the legislators will have been developed by the identified disciples.
3. The disciples will have advocated the two focus issues with their legislators and governor in a consistent manner throughout the legislative session.
4. Legislation will have been passed to adequately fund Early Childhood Development, so all Minnesota children will have access to Head Start, Early Childhood Family Education, School Readiness, or Sliding Fee Child Care services.
5. Legislation will have been passed to adequately fund MinnesotaCare, Medical Assistance, General Assistance Medical Care, and the Child Health Security Act.

Cluster roster

From the beginning of the formation of the clusters, a major challenge was communication—how to stay in contact, how to notify people about cluster gatherings, how to give current legislative updates on the two focus issues. With limited staff time to devote to any one area of responsibility, the simple answer to the communication challenge was e-mail. The cluster roster was updated religiously. Action alerts, researched by a knowledgeable part-time staff member, were sent out weekly, especially toward the end of the legislative session. An example of one of these action alerts follows:

Action Needed:
Write to the Governor, House Speaker, and/or Senate Majority Leader.

Message: (Use any or all of these points in your own setting)

- We should not cut people off health care or child care to balance the budget. We can fund the needs of our state by restoring the 1999 income tax levels or by other fair and honest means. It's time to compromise and get the job done. Seize the opportunity to invest in Minnesota families.
- Minnesotans prioritize funding MinnesotaCare at 2003 levels. Do not cut thirty thousand more people off the program.
- Minnesota cannot afford NOT to invest abundantly in our youngest children. Please expand the child care assistance program so that every working family can access quality child care, remove the freeze on child care provider rates, and invest in ECFE (Early Childhood Family Education), Head Start, School Readiness, and the MELF (Minnesota Early Learning Foundation).

Individual clusters

Each of the eight clusters had its own facilitator(s)—someone who led the work of that particular cluster and also served on the now-expanded Advocacy subgroup. Some of the clusters met on a monthly basis to plan their legislative visits, to write letters, to discuss issues in their particular area, and to invite additional congregations into the work. Others kept in contact only by e-mail. All of the clusters worked to identify the twelve disciples in each legislative district in their cluster. Some clusters were responsible for only one legislative district; others related to three or four districts. The location of the churches involved in each particular cluster was the determining factor.

From casseroles and green Jell-O to "The Hill"

Working to end poverty and stepping into a messy legislative process can be serious business, so much so that, in planning the cluster gathering for March 31, one of the leaders suggested we interject some humor and fun. The planning group had already determined that one goal for that gathering would be to face our fears of getting involved in the legislative process. After all, for many of us, this step into the public arena was new and a bit daunting. Thus came the creative idea for a skit—improv (but rehearsed improv)—to depict a legislative visit gone awry: an uncooperative legislator who knew how to avoid giving a direct answer to any question, an aid who was practiced in the art of distraction, and three faithful visitors who were naïve and in awe of being in the state capitol as well as committed to making their points. The result of the skit was laughter, a sense of fun, and, most important, some valuable learning about what to do and what not to do when making a legislative visit.

We are one community

We knew we needed one last all-cluster gathering for this legislative session. We knew we would want to assess our work and either celebrate or weep together. We chose June 15 for that gathering, assuming that even if there would be a special session, that it would have ended by that date. It had not. Nevertheless the gathering went on with great enthusiasm—and even fun.

The theme for the gathering was "We Are One Community" and the purpose of the gathering was threefold:

- To assess our work and give a legislative status report on our two issues
- To celebrate the work toward ending poverty and the joy of new and deepening relationships
- To discuss future plans for the upcoming year

At this gathering we also welcomed new congregations and several new developing clusters into our joint work. Two additional Minnesota synods were represented as well.

Plan for the year ahead

The draft of the plan was presented at the June 15 gathering. Facilitators led table discussions to give feedback and responses to the plan. Participants chose the arenas in which they wanted to be involved. The Advocacy subgroup will now continue to incorporate these further ideas and suggestions into future plans.

The five major parts of the plan for the coming year are:
- Expanding the network to all of our region or state
- Upcoming legislative session
- Upcoming election process
- Education about the role of faith within civil society
- Involvement and empowerment of people living in poverty

Education/Service subgroup

With a slower start-up, the Education/Service subgroup has, in recent months, made great strides in their work. Several of the team members, as well as I, have made numerous presentations on poverty in adult forums—from a budget simulation process called "Could You Live on This? Making It on a Low-Wage Budget" to Ruby Payne's "Framework for Understanding Poverty."

The subgroup also has continued to involve many congregations in the work of Habitat for Humanity, building one synod house per year for the last several years.

Now, in addition to these efforts, the Education/Service subgroup has developed a "Discipleship Walk" to engage congregations in a four-step service and learning experience. In this pilot, participants will be involved in education for action, a transforming volunteer experience, reflection, and opportunities for ongoing commitment.

Far more . . .

Months ago we stumbled onto what has become the theme Bible passage for the entire process of *Ending Poverty: A Biblical Moral Mandate within Civil Society.* What is perhaps most interesting is that the verses do not have a direct connection to one of the many Bible passages that speak about poverty and care for those living in poverty. However, this benediction has permeated our discussions and our planning, and we believe it:

> *Now to [God] who by the power at work within us is able to accomplish abundantly far more than we can ask or imagine, to [God] be glory in the church and in Christ Jesus to all generations, forever and ever. Amen (Ephesians 3:20-21).*